T0128142

REFLECTIONS
OF A
BABY BOOMER

GROWING UP IN THE 50'S PLUS
OTHER RELATED ESSAYS AND JOURNALS

BRUCE LIDSTROM

Order this book online at www.trafford.com
or email orders@trafford.com

Most Trafford titles are also available at major online book retailers.

© Copyright 2019 Bruce Lidstrom.
All rights reserved. No part of this publication may be reproduced, stored in a retrieval
system, or transmitted, in any form or by any means, electronic, mechanical, photocopying,
recording, or otherwise, without the written prior permission of the author.

Print information available on the last page.

ISBN: 978-1-4907-9790-8 (sc)
ISBN: 978-1-4907-9789-2 (hc)

Library of Congress Control Number: 2019916442

Because of the dynamic nature of the Internet, any web addresses or links contained in
this book may have changed since publication and may no longer be valid. The views
expressed in this work are solely those of the author and do not necessarily reflect the
views of the publisher, and the publisher hereby disclaims any responsibility for them.

Trafford rev. 10/30/2019

 www.trafford.com
North America & international
toll-free: 1 888 232 4444 (USA & Canada)
fax: 812 355 4082

PART 1

50 STATES

Long before the term Bucket List was popular, I had a goal of visiting all 50 states. It may have started when I was a kid playing with a states puzzle. I pretty much knew all the states. Since my mom was from the east coast I heard about places like Pennsylvania, New York and New Jersey. Everyone knew Florida and Texas. In 1959 we added the last two states, Alaska and Hawaii so we learned about the "lower 48" as a byproduct of those additions. When we added the new states, a new star was added to the US flag. The flag with 49 stars did not last long as Hawaii followed soon after. Living in Seattle I was not exactly well centered to visit most of the states.

I did not realize that it would take 60 years before I visited them all, but I did make my goal. So, without fanfare or celebration I landed in Honolulu in 2009 to make number 50. I had been to Alaska in 2005.

I got started toward my interstate travel slowly. Born in Washington the second state I visited was Oregon. One of my dad's sisters lived in Portland and I recall visiting at a very young age. Probably before age 5. California was my third state and that first visit came in 1959. At that rate it was going to take a while to see them all. Once my younger siblings got a little older we started taking longer family vacations.

In 1960 we did a very memorable trip. I added Idaho, Montana, Wyoming, Colorado, New Mexico, Arizona and Utah. We had friends we stayed with in Denver and we visited several National Parks. Those were Yellowstone, Grand Teton, Mesa Verdi, Grand Canyon, and Zion. Not only do I still have the family pictures of that trip, but also the maps my dad got from AAA. Our routes were drawn out and I can see which roads we took. The interstate highways had not been built yet so we traveled the older US highways. So, at age 11 my state total was at 10. Good progress.

We followed with another long trip in 1961. That year we went all the way to Ironwood, Michigan on the Upper Peninsula. We headed east out of Seattle and North Dakota was my first new state. We then hit Minnesota, Wisconsin, Michigan, and then South Dakota on the return. I was now at 15 states. I did feel that my Michigan visit was kind of cheating. While I was officially in the state it was a very small area of the Upper Peninsula bordering Wisconsin and Lake Superior. Our visit to New Mexico the prior year was also brief as we just cut off the northwest corner. We did stop in Gallup at a store and had lunch at the city park. (Which was also the town cemetery.)

In 1964 we did another western swing going to Nevada. A state we had missed on our other trips. At age 15 my state total was 16. It would stay that way for over 10 more years. However, in 1967 I did something totally different. I had graduated from high school and had a summer job with the Washington State Dept. of Highways. The week before I went away to college I flew to Montreal for Expo '67. A huge World's Fair. I first flew to Vancouver and then across Canada to Toronto and then Montreal. I was now counting Canadian Provinces in my travels I visited British Columbia, Ontario, and Quebec on that trip. However, that did nothing to add to my state totals.

My journey to make all 50 states resumed in 1976. Connie and I had been married three years. I had two weeks of vacation and we traveled to Lawrenceburg, Indiana to attend Connie's Grandparents 50th wedding anniversary. That was in late August 1976. By then I was also traveling a fair amount on my job going to San Francisco, Los Angeles, Phoenix, and Spokane.

Connie, her sister Debbie and I took a mid-night flight to Chicago and then an early morning flight from there to Cincinnati. Lawrenceburg was just across the Ohio River from the Covington, Kentucky airport.

After the family reunion we were given use of the Cotton family station wagon for the next two weeks. We drove all the way to Boston and then back across the country to Seattle. Lots of driving and lots of sights. We left Lawrenceburg with Bob and his dog Erin. We dropped him off at Cornell University in Ithaca, New York. Then on to Connecticut, where Connie's Uncle Jim and family lived. From there we took day trips to Newport, Rhode Island, and Boston. So now all the way back across the country.

After a return through Ithaca we stopped at Niagara Falls, went down through Ohio and back to see the grandparents in Indiana. From there it was two days to get to Denver, where we had friends. From there on to Seattle. I added 11 new states bringing my total to 27. Now I was more than half way to my goal. Illinois, Kentucky, Indiana, Ohio, Pennsylvania, New York, Connecticut, Massachusetts, Rhode Island, Missouri, and Kansas.

Connie's brother was married at West Point, New York in 1979. We flew out from California, where we were then living, and added New Jersey to my list. I was at 28. If I recall we had a landing at Dulles, in Virginia, but did not get off the plane so I did not count Virginia at the time.

About this time I started traveling more for my job. I would occasionally visit a new state, even if was just to change planes. I counted those as states at the time and did get back to all those states and do some actual visiting. Some of the states I knocked off my list up to 1986 were Texas, Oklahoma, Georgia, West Virginia, Vermont, and New Hampshire. I would fly in to teach a class or attend a meeting and then move on to the next state. I was not keeping an "up to the minute" tally but looking back I realize by then my count was at 34.

Then we moved to the Mid-west. First to Ohio and then in 1987 to Indiana. Now I was better situated to visit the eastern half of the country. On the drive to Ohio, I did not add any new states, but started keeping track of states for my kids who drove with me. Yes, Kristin, we did drive through Wyoming. We stayed in Rock Springs.

I have lost track of business travel at this point. I probably added Florida which put my total at 35. We took a couple of family vacations between 1987 and 1990. We had a spring break trip to Florida where I was able to add Tennessee to the list. Then we drove to Maine for a week on the coast. In 1991 we added Delaware (although just the short distance on I-95), Maryland, Washington DC (not part of the actual count), and Virginia. My total was now at 40.

We first visited Iowa to attend a week-long AAU baseball tournament in Des Moines in 1993. So, my total was at 41. Likewise, we had a couple of tournaments in Omaha in the mid 90's taking Nebraska off the list.

By this point there were now just a few pockets of states I had not seen yet. In the west only Nebraska had been missed. I felt just being to Omaha was kind of cheating as it was right on the border to Iowa. In the east the Carolinas. In the south Alabama, Mississippi, Arkansas, and Louisiana. Also, Alaska and Hawaii.

So now we would have to make a conscious effort to see the remaining states. Even if we had to go out of our way to get there. I think by now I had probably flown through Charlotte, North Carolina a few times. However, Connie's brother Jim had moved to the state and we took a vacation to visit him around 2002. I now added North and South Carolina to the list. Six to go. About this same time, I attended a convention in New Orleans, so Louisiana was off the list. Just five left.

I took a couple of Civil War battlefield trips around 2000 to 2002. One found us in Memphis after visiting Shiloh in SW Tennessee. We were right on the Mississippi and I talked the group to going across the bridge into Arkansas. I just need four more. I felt better about Nebraska as well as we drove all the way across on I-80 in 2003.

In 2005 we flew to Seattle and did an Alaskan cruise. While mostly at sea we had stops in Juneau and Sitka. Then in 2007 we had a business trip to Arkansas and took a very indirect route to get there going through northern Alabama and Mississippi. 48 and 49. So now we deserved a really nice vacation and did our Hawaii trip in 2009. I remember having dinner the first night there in Kona and telling some people I had just made all 50 states.

So now what?

In doing all this travel Connie did many of the states with me. However, she is stuck at 49 as she had only missed Oklahoma. We were just a few miles away in NW Arkansas and didn't realize at the time she needed only that state. We will make it there for some reason.

Also, I said I felt guilty about only hitting a small portion of some states. Well I have now been to 47 states more than once. However, my time in Delaware is still limited to the interstate and rail lines. The only states I have not been to more than once are Maine, Alaska, and Hawaii. There are two "lower 48" states that I did not drive to get there. Louisiana and Texas. I have probably been to Texas 10 times (not counting plane changes in Dallas) and I have never driven there.

To enhance some of my visits I took a 31 state Amtrak trip in 2015. From Minnesota I went to Boston, then Florida, back to DC, to New Orleans, across the south to LA and up the coast to Portland and Seattle. Then back to Minnesota. I saw a lot of new country going across the south, especially Texas.

I've made all 50 and then some.

CARS

Kids grew up in the 50's and 60's with a thing for cars. Even now boomers can look at many cars from the 50's and know the make, model, and year for most the popular cars of the day. Foreign made cars were very rare, with the Volkswagen beetle probably being the most common. However, cars all the kids knew were Fords, Chevys, Dodges, Pontiacs, Oldsmobile's, and then maybe Mercury's and some cars that were soon to be extinct like Hudson's, and Studebakers.

I wish I had asked my dad what my first car ride was in. What car did he have when he drove me home from the hospital? Was it his 1946 Ford or a new 1949 Ford? I was born in December of 1948 and the 49's were probably already out. I just don't know when he bought his. He usually got new cars right when new ones came out. At some point I need to look at pictures and see what car might be in the background around that time.

During World War II no new cars were made. All the manufacturing went into the war effort. The auto plants that had made cars were converted into the manufacturing of planes, jeeps, tanks, and everything else. With so many young men away in uniform there was a whole generation that were not around to buy cars anyway. Even those who had cars were limited in their use due to gas rationing. My mom's family never had a car. Production of cars started up right after the war, in 1946. Within a few years all the military men were getting civilian jobs and buying their first cars.

As kids we really never knew how much a car cost. Very few families had more than one. Dad took the car to work and we ran our errands during the day by walking, riding bikes, or taking the bus. We always had a nice family car. But, by the late 50's my dad bought a pick-up truck and that was what he used for work. The car sat in the garage and my mom still never drove. Not until I started driving in 1965-66 was that car used during the day. And even that was very limited.

Some high school kids had cars, but really not many. The high school student parking lot was only a fraction of the size that my kids' school had to offer. Growing up there were always "big kids" in the neighborhood who had cars. They were always working on them. Many teenagers were after school mechanics continually trying to get their car running after they rebuilt an engine or something. We would hang around some of those guys until their patience ran short, sometimes with us and sometimes with their car. Their cars had to be loud with noisy exhaust and tires that squealed when pulling out. Police tended to be far more tolerant of these cars and kids than they would be today.

Our two-car garage, behind the house, often times acted as a "shop". We had tools to do a lot of our own work. Oil changes, new brakes, spark plugs, and tire rotation were all done frequently and usually followed by a car wash. We had a barrel to dispose of used motor oil and my dad had it emptied every few years. After we kids started college and had our own cars there could be quite a bit of work to keep all the cars running to my dad's approval. As long as I still lived close to my folks I would do my oil changes in our back alley.

We had snow tires on their own wheels which we kept in the rafters of the garage. Dad had rigged a pulley system to make it easy to get them down and up again. One car I owned even had studded snow tires. They became illegal in later years because of the damage they could do to the road surface. Basically, they had small spikes to grip the road in ice and snow. Snow tires themselves were only good for a few thousand miles and they would lose their deep tread. We only put them on the cars when it was going to snow. Then we took them off when the snow melted. By the early 70's my dad had advanced to a one-ton pick-up. We really needed the pulley system for those oversize tires. It didn't take us long to change tires on a couple of vehicles when we knew snow was coming.

The most detailed work I remember doing was brakes, replacing a cracked exhaust manifold, and spark plug wires. The spark plug wires would not have been a big deal, but my dad found a way to get the replacement parts really cheap. The spark plug wires came in one long spool and we had to cut each wire and then insert the terminals. One end to the plug, the other to the distributor. Like I said they were cheap and my V-8 was probably only running on six cylinders when I finished. After all that we then had to go out and buy wires made for that car.

That same car (a 69 Plymouth Fury III retired highway patrol car) had heater hoses that were springing leaks. Buy new hoses? No way. My dad just bought me some copper tubing and clamps. Every time the hose sprung a leak I would cut it in that spot, insert the tubing and clamp them tight. Of course, I had to also carry extra radiator fluid and water in case my leak was sprung somewhere on the open road. (Which happened a couple times). I wonder what a new heater hose would have cost?

Now days I hardly lift the hood of a car. Usually just to check or top off the oil and washer fluid. That's it. It's too hard to even change oil and you just can't pour the old oil down the drain. I'm sure those who live on farms still do a lot of their own work, but cars run on computers now and the average person does not invest in the equipment to run basic diagnostics. Needless to say, my kids have probably never changed oil in a car or taken off a tire.

The reason I can recall so many of the 50's makes and models is that my dad bought a new car every couple of years. If he didn't our neighbors did. Jack had Buick's on one side of our house and on the other side Chevy's. After the 1949 Ford I recall (with a fairly certain degree of accuracy) we had a 1951 Pontiac, 1952 Olds, 1954 Olds, 1956 Olds, 1959 Ford station wagon (all those cars were two toned in color). Then back to Oldsmobile's in 1960 and then 1962. For some reason we switched to a Buick in 1964. A 1964 that we only had one year. (My dad would try new cars but didn't keep them if they didn't measure up). That was the car I learned to drive. Now it is getting foggy. I think my dad squeezed in one more Oldsmobile before we switched to Cadillac's in 1968. By then I was away at school and had my own cars so what Dad had was not as meaningful to me. However, he drove Cadillac's until he couldn't drive any more. Then he kept the car so I would have something to drive when I visited Seattle.

I had mentioned trucks. From the late 50's when my dad bought a used Ford pickup we always had a truck. He liked the utility of having a truck and he could park in truck loading zones in downtown Seattle as part of his job of fixing typewriters. By the mid 60's he had bought a camper unit that rode in the bed of the pickup and he had the trucks and a camper up till the 90's.

Most kids today do not have the opportunity of learning how to drive a stick shift, (manual transmission.) Three of my four kids just looked at me and said "why would anyone want to do that?" The other only drove a stick until he got married and his wife didn't like it. Go figure. My dad's trucks were manual for some time, so I learned both manual and automatic at the same time. Therefore, driving a stick came naturally. I can go a couple of years without manually shifting and when I do get in a car that requires shifting it all comes back. Clutch, shift, and go again.

Many other features of cars have changed since the 50's. The high beam switch used to be a button on the floor. All the turn signal arm did was turn on the turn signal. When they moved the high beam to a fingertip control people joked that old folks still had to turn on high beams with their foot getting their leg stuck trying to push the turn signal lever.

There was no such thing as washer fluid, car stereo systems, air conditioning, automatic thermostats, padded dashboards, air bags, and seat belts. Seatbelts? Yes, cars had no seat belts.

Look up accident figures from the 50's as a ratio to miles driven. Even minor accidents could produce serious injuries. The steering column did not collapse in a head on accident. Instead it might be impaled into the driver's chest. Dash boards were metal. No padding. Ashtrays were spaced where today we have cup holders.

Music? We had AM radio. But, that was where we heard all the great songs from the 50's and 60's. "KJR Seattle, Channel 95". That was 950 on the AM dial and was a top 40 station. Parents might listen to the more conservative network affiliated stations that had traffic reports and more news. Their music was what was left over when rock and roll debuted in the 50's. Pat Boone maybe.

We thought high tech was automated air vents. Instead of pulling open a vent for fresh or cool air I recall when my dad's Olds had button that opened vents and a fan that could hurry the air along.

Safety was a consideration for the future. The government had to mandate many of the safety features that we take for granted. And the auto manufacturers pushed back trying to delay the inevitable. By the 60's cars were equipped with front seat belts. They may have been an option at first. They were just lab straps like you have on airplanes today. There was nothing for the back seats. After all you had the seat back of the front seats to protect you if thrown forward.

My dad had been in an accident as a kid where his whole family was crowded in the car. A couple were thrown out and there were some broken bones. I'm not sure if that was the reason or not, but he first bought rear seat belts for one of his early 60 cars. So, we were strapped in to the back seats before virtually anyone else in the country. As kids it seemed normal and we didn't resist. When we rode in the front we wore one so having them in the back made sense. I don't recall my dad ever not buckling up.

However, my dad was also frugal. One year when we traded cars he saved money by not ordering rear seat belts. Instead we took the ones out of the car we were trading in (he had installed them anyway) and put them in the back seat of the new car. So what that the colors didn't match the seats. We stayed safe.

Over all those years I was never personally involved in any serious accidents and my dad had only one with one of his trucks. He was not injured. We may have had some hard stops, but the seat belts did their job. As an adult I could never drive in anyone else's car without belting up. It was just the normal thing to do.

Likewise, there were no kid seat for babies and toddlers. Small babies where held by mom. Once a kid could sit up there may have been a stool of some type so they could see out the windows, but no kids were strapped in. Now even people who refuse to wear seat belts will probably make sure their small children are secure. The middle of the back seat. That allows older siblings to have a window seat.

Show me a picture of a car from the 50's and early 60's and I will know the manufacturer and be within a year of the model year.

1957 was the first year for big fins. 1958 saw the introduction of four head lights instead of two. Most cars changed things yearly, so it was easy to distinguish a 56 from a 57 and a 58 and so on. If my dad didn't buy a new car every year we went out to the dealerships and looked at all the new ones the week they came out.

New cars came out in September just after school started. Every year you would see the searchlight cutting across the sky at night pinpointing the dealerships location. The car dealers rented WWII military surplus search lights used to spot enemy aircraft during air raids. Now they announced the new car model years. And like a moth that is attracted to the bright porch light we were drawn to the local Chevy, Ford or Buick dealer to look at new cars. I think most of the dealers knew my dad and knew it would be a tough sell to get him away from his Olds. By the late 60's he was invited to Champaign showings when the new Cadillacs came out. He and my mom hardly ever missed one.

Prejudices that were formed when my dad was a kid carried with him his whole life. He was a Ford guy for trucks and General Motors for passenger cars. Except for Chevrolet. They were always a "bucket of bolts". Even though Buick, Chevy, Olds and Pontiac were all made from the basic same molds he had no use for Chevy's. However, even they were superior to the Japanese cars. Even when they started building really good cars he would not listen. It would have been an ultimate insult if any of us kids were to have bought a Japanese car. German would be okay, but not from Japan. In 2011 I bought a new GMC Sierra Pick up. When I told my brother he said, "Bucket of bolts hey?" I had to laugh.

ELEMENTARY SCHOOL

When baby boomers started going to school in the late 1940's and early 50's a huge expansion of facilities was necessary all over the country. New schools had to be built or old ones expanded. The school I attended from 1954 to 1961 (K to 6) had only four class rooms around 1950. By the time I started Kindergarten in September of 1954 there were 12 classrooms. By the time I was in the 5th grade there were an additional 7 portable classrooms set up on the playground. My sixth-grade class (the only year we had a year-book) had about 80 students. We had two full sixth grade classes and another that was split with 5th grade.

Based on that I am guessing our school had about 600 students by 1960 as compared to only four rooms in 1950.

Two things happened to our neighborhood. First, hundreds of homes were built after the war, starting in the late 40's. Prior to that our neighborhood was woods and small farm plots. While part of Seattle, it was probably the last area developed. Then every one of those new houses had a family with an average of three kids.

While we were already well removed from the old one-room school house it seemed that some of our teachers may have started out teaching under that environment. My kindergarten teacher retired in 1957 so I am guessing she started teaching during the First World War, 1917. We did have modern stand-alone desks. It was not until I went to Junior High in 1961 that I actually saw the old row desks where the seat lifted up and there was a hole for the ink well. That school building was built in 1929 and still had some of the original furniture. However, we'll talk about junior high a different time.

Grade school became a comfortable environment even though I was usually scared of some of my teachers. I had only women teachers and they were very strict. They seemed to have no qualms about embarrassing someone. "I don't know" was not an acceptable answer, which seemed illogical to me if I didn't know.

The school yard doubled as our neighborhood play ground after school, on weekends, and in summer. Older boys were always playing basketball and we played hours of softball and baseball on an asphalt field that had the bases painted on. A backstop kept most foul balls from going in the street next to the playground. Then there was the "lower fields" which ramps took you down to. There were football goalposts and a very hard, dry clay surface. We played more baseball there as well as football pickup games.

The two ramps crisscrossed in the middle and turned into narrow sled shoots when it snowed. I can remember two injuries incurred sledding down those ramps. There was a slight jog where the two ramps intersected. I think we were doing a train (hooking our feet in the sleigh behind us and I was pulled into a fence post which hit with my leg. I was afraid it was broke. My friends had to pull me home on my sleigh. Since we were never taken to the doctor for virtually anything, I was put to bed in hopes that it got better. I missed one of my few days of school the next day, but slowly got my leg use back and a big bruise.

That was in second grade. A couple of years later we had more snow. I learned my lesson and figured the best way to go down was solo. I had a great run down the steep ramp and kept my speed up out into the playfield where I hit the metal goal post head first. You know the sound a metal post makes when something hard hits it? Well that is what I heard. Of course, we could never tell our parents what I had done as we were not supposed to be there in the first place. I didn't feel like sledding much more that day. I was probably lucky I did not break my neck.

While throwing snowballs was forbidden while at school, we did have one "organized" snowball fight on the lower field during school. I recall how excited I was to finally be able to take out some of my friends with snowballs. With the first volley I took a snow ball to the nose which quickly started bleeding and my snow ball war was over. I probably was not the only injury and we never did that again. Meanwhile, I got busted by the principal one day while walking home from school. (I only had to go one block to get home) and got caught throwing a snowball at a friend. I was sent to the Principals office with about 10 other kids. So, what kind of a person was I going to turn out to be if I blatantly disregarded rules? I'd probably end up in prison. Problem was I believed Miss Young. I was bad. Threw a snow ball.

The school yard had a thick yellow line down the middle to divide the boys' side from the girls. We could only play on our side. However, my portable classroom was on the girls' side. When we got to school in the morning there was already kick ball games being played, among other things, and we could play until the first bell. However, if we brought our lunch or had books, we would drop them off on the portable steps and go back and play. You guessed it. I was busted again for being on the girl's side of the playground. Off to the Principals office again. As I was thinking up my logical defense we were simply released back to our classes when Miss Young returned. I think my teacher may have been informed and said something in my defense since it never came up again.

Meanwhile, we did learn things. We did not know what a computer was. Likewise, there was only one TV in the school and I only remember watching it for Kennedy's inaugural in January 1961 and again that May when Alan Sheppard became the first American to go into space. We did see movies (films), and it seems film strips were very common. Those would have lessons in math or English. Film strips did not have individual slides but a roll that was advanced through the projector.

I also recall listening on the radio for some special lessons. The Standard School Broadcast would have a different theme each year. The shows were probably about one-half hour and entertaining. A nice departure from the teacher. Seems one year (maybe 3rd grade) the topic was classical music. We would listen to the work of a composer and were supposed to be inspired to color a picture of some type. I never made the connection as to how a piece of classical music was supposed to inspire me to some artistic endeavor.

However, in 5th grade the series was on National Parks. A real park Ranger and a guest hosted the show each week and I loved those programs. I could color a picture of Old Faithful, or of mountains, or a rock bridge in Utah. I wanted to visit every park I learned about and over the next 5-6 years our family visited many of the western parks. One memory that has stayed with me was hearing the song "Ghost Riders in the Sky". I think the featured park that week was Big Bend in Texas and the Ranger who was a guest that week had written the song.

I still like the song and can remember the first time I ever heard it in the 5th grade. Mrs. Rice was my teacher that year.

As mentioned, the teachers could be very strict. I recall Mrs. Rice breaking a ruler over the wrist of Jimmy Dunlap. Of course, we all laughed, which probably didn't help Jimmy. Older kids might be punished by "swats". A tennis shoe was the weapon Mr. Talmadge used. Throwing snow balls after school or being on the girls' side of the playground apparently did not warrant a swatting, but there were a few students who seemed to find plenty of other infractions to bring out the shoe.

There were several kids who I was in every class with until 6th grade. Larry Prescott, Bob Sepulveda, and Sue MacKinnon and a few others always got the same teachers. I was actually upset when they spread us out in sixth grade. Even though a year later we would totally be mixed up in junior high and be joined by kids from about 7or 8 other elementary schools.

Age wise I was in the older half of the kids in my class and was therefore assigned to afternoon kindergarten. Miss Williams was my teacher and as I said had already been teaching for about 40 years. As kids that meant nothing to us. She was old like our grandmothers were, but very nice. Being in the afternoon class we no longer needed naps at school. The morning kids did have a short nap period so of course we called them "Kindergarten Babies". However, many of the older kids in school picked on all the kindergarteners regardless of morning or afternoon. We were targets. A member of the safety patrol led us each day to the street crossing where other safety patrols directed our crossing. At the next intersection we were on our own, but the three main intersections around the school had the patrols.

The year I started kindergarten was the year that Boeing first flew the 707. The plane that would be the first jet passenger airliner. The original two-tone brown plane was seen over the city very frequently and the distinct whine of the engines sent people outside to watch it fly over. One afternoon we could hear the plane approaching the airspace over Genesee Hill. Miss Williams had our entire class hurry into the courtyard outside our room to watch the plane as if none of us had ever seen it before. The 707 was low and the four engines had a whistling tone to them. Miss Williams then proceed to tell us that noise was important as it meant the plane was "on the beam". Now, I was only six, but I think I realized that some of us might actually know more about 707's than our teacher. I think a few of us just laughed among ourselves. The next time I go to a class reunion I have to see if anyone else remembers that incident the way I do, if at all.

Second grade was somewhat interesting for me in that I was in a second/third grade combination. While the second graders worked on our own, we often got to hear the third-grade lesson. I was particularly interested in learning cursive writing. I would practice the word "*little*" all the time. That was an easy cursive word to make. However, my early introduction to cursive did little to help my penmanship. I got mostly C's in handwriting. I liked handwriting about as much as I did coloring pictures while listening to some classical music piece.

One of my biggest scares came as I was walking home from school from the last day of 2nd grade. We were told that we were not allowed to open our report cards. We were to only give them to our parents. However, I peeked enough to see that I was to report the next school year to room 9. The scare was that room 9 had been the room I had just finished 2nd grade in. I was sure Miss Reader had flunked me. About then one of my friends asked if I had Reader again for 3rd grade. Seems he did. Then I realized that I had advanced to 3rd grade, but just had the same teacher. Not a big thrill, but a relief that I had passed.

My next-door neighbor was a 4th grade teacher at our school. In school she was Mrs. Jackson, but over the back fence "Betty" was okay. In school every kid was petrified of Mrs. Jackson, and they thought it must be terrible to live next door to such a mean teacher. But, outside of school I actually liked Betty and her husband Jack was always very nice to me. Starting at age 12 I took care of their yard, by mowing and doing all the yard work when they went on vacation. Almost all my early teen spending money came from that job.

However, at school things were all business and I probably behaved better then I might otherwise as I didn't want her telling my mom something I did. I'm sure there were situations, but nothing serious that I remember. I also had a younger sister and brother at Genesee by the time I was in 4th grade so my mom had three of us to keep track of.

At the end of the 4th grade I was called in to Mrs. Jackson's room. That had never happened before, and I was very nervous. She asked if I was interested in being on the safety patrol. Wear a belt and had a red flag and say "Ready…. Walk". That was very cool, and I was secretly very thankful she considered me. Then a year later she asked if I would be the First Lieutenant. Bob Sepulveda was Captain and Sue Supplee was a Second Lieutenant. We supervised a squad of three teams (six kids) who worked three of the intersections around the school. Then there were two kindergarten patrols which led the children from their classroom to the closest street crossing. I got a badge on my belt and a white helmet that invited all my friends to see just how hard my head was.

At our 40th class reunion, Bob, Sue and I shared some of our memories of the safety patrol. Seemed it was memorable of each of us. Captain Bob had to do a monthly report. For some reason I always helped him and we each got out of class to do the report. It was not until the end of the school year that Mrs. Jackson realized we each were out of class. By then it was too late to do anything about that. At the time of the same class reunion I was visiting a high school friend who had gone to a different elementary school. In looking at his year book I realized that all their patrols were boys. Turns out Mrs. Jackson was ahead of her time in including the girls and even having a girl officer.

Grade school in the 50's was still in the shadow of World War II. While we were born afterwards our parents served in the war or someone in their family did. My 4th grade teacher lost her husband in the war and she had two teenage kids she was raising alone. Every Wednesday at noon we heard the air raid siren test. We were usually home at lunch when that occurred, but many of our kid games were war related. In addition to fire drills and earthquake drills (under our desks), we also had air raid drills. If we had coats at school, we took our coat and laid down on the floor of a long windowless hallway with the coats over our heads. It was kind of scary. Even more so in that some of us knew that we were not likely to be bombed by conventional bombs, but the atomic type that ended our war with Japan.

Our enemy was Russia. Actually, the Soviet Union, but we always referred to them as Russia. We were not friends with China either, but they were not considered a threat to deliver a nuclear weapon to Seattle. Our parents told us that Seattle was a target because Boeing Aircraft was there. Many of the bombers build in World War II were built in Seattle. Our waterfront was the closest to Asia and just across Puget Sound was a huge navy yard in Bremerton. They had the biggest dry dock in the world. Or so we believed. There were a lot of other military presence in the Puget Sound area in those days and still is. Enough that we considered ourselves a target.

That threat could be a big concern for a child in grade school. As carefree as grade school was, we all knew there was a real world out there that didn't like our way of life. Personally, I always liked seeing military presence in our area as I felt we were being protected. B-47's, B-52's and KC 135 tanker planes were often seen at Boeing Field while they underwent some new work.

Mrs. Jackson doubled as the girls PE teacher. While that usually did not affect the boys there was one time of the year that all the kids did the same activity. Square dancing. Yes, square dancing. That culminated with an all school dance in the school yard that parents (moms) could come and see. Since most mom's stayed home, they were our target audience. Each grade had a dance they would learn. I must admit right here that I hated square dancing. In fact, I had no use for virtually any dancing at all. I blame square dancing for that. I never went to school dances in high school as I could not break the connection to square dancing. On top of that I recall one year being partnered with a girl I was just not wild about. Holding hands with someone you were not attracted to was torture for me. What if other kids teased me? They didn't as everyone was in the same boat and one year, I do recall being partnered with one girl who I did find acceptable. Even now I don't want to name names. Someone I know could read this.

We also had a music teacher. Mrs. Jones was one of the 4th grade teachers. Our class periodically went in to sing. She played the piano and we learned just about every song of Americana possible. "Old Susanna", "Good Bye, Old Paint", "Way Down Upon the Swannee River", etc. We had a decent Christmas Choir and could still do religious songs in 1960. It was fun doing those songs that we would also sing in church. "O Holy Night" was my favorite for the Christmas show we did for the parents. (That was an evening show so Dads could go).

We did not learn any foreign language that I recall. We did one field trip in Kindergarten (zoo) and maybe one in 4th grade. (A Seattle Harbor Tour). I don't recall any special programs for bright kids, however, usually the slow students were put together, so we all knew who they were. I never thought it was right how they were identified for the possible teasing by everyone else.

Mr. Bogardus was the science teacher for the older kids. He was well liked. A very large man he could be very entertaining. He addressed kids very formally, "Master Lidstrom" can you tell us......?" He also could reduce someone to dust with a well phrased comment.

We had no minorities at our school. I can think of one Japanese family in the later years. No blacks, no Hispanics. There was one family who moved into our neighborhood from Sweden. In saying all of that we thought we were normal. Religion wise I don't believe there were any Jewish families in our neighborhood. We didn't know what a Jewish person was. Maybe we would see them on TV, but even television in those days was pretty much like what we saw at home.

Somehow, we were all prepared to advance to junior high and beyond.

NATIONAL PARKS

From about the 5th grade on I had an infatuation with our National Parks. From our house in Seattle, where I grew up, you can see two national parks, Rainier and Olympic. In fact, on a really clear day we may also be able to see a third, the North Cascades. We could see Mt. Baker, which is just outside that park. I recall taking day trips to Mt. Rainier. It was only a couple of hours away even though it loomed so large out our kitchen window. However, I do not recall ever actually visiting Olympic National Park. While we could see it on any clear day from Seattle there were really no roads through the park. Probably the most popular drive that goes into the park from the North is to see the view from Hurricane Ridge. I'm sure I was there but don't remember it. I finally had a chance to make that drive and a hike in the summer of 2016.

Dad wanted to go to Yellowstone in 1959, but he spent so much money on gear that he could not afford a long vacation. However, we had a good "shakedown cruise". That year we went to Crater Lake in Oregon and then into northern California to Shasta and Lassen National Park. We had a 1959 Ford Station Wagon for that trip. Our tent could sleep the entire family, but it was crowded. I recall sleeping in the back of the station wagon. One morning in Crater Lake I awoke just as it was getting light and several deer were going through the camp site right next to our car. They did not detect me at all in the car.

As it turned out it was probably a good thing that we missed Yellowstone in 1959 as a major earthquake hit the area that summer. There is a good chance we would have been in that area the week of the earthquake. A high school and college class mate of mine was there and it was pretty scary. Crater Lake was magnificent. Such blue water and it was interesting learning about how there used to be a big mountain which had blown its top leaving the crater. It is the deepest lake in the country at about 2000 feet. In the west there was a theme of making volcanoes the site of National Parks. Rainier, Crater Lake, and Lassen were all volcanoes.

In 1960 we started out on a family vacation around June 20 and had our first visit to Yellowstone. We did not camp in Yellowstone. In fact, it was so cold on June 21st (first day of summer, right?) we drove through snow flurries in Montana heading toward Yellowstone. We stayed at a very old motel in Gardner, which is at the NW entrance to the park. No TV or radio. That night was a heavyweight fight featuring Floyd Patterson and Ingmar Johansson. We had trouble getting a signal even on our car radio and another motel guest invited us into his car which had somewhat better reception than ours. Roughing it!

Dad never made reservations for anything. I don't think we could get a camping spot in Yellowstone. But Grand Teton Park, just to the south, had spots so we camped there. We were right next to Jackson Lake. That night we were kept awake by bears in the water close to our camp site. In Yellowstone we saw Old Faithful and many, many bears. I make note of that as it is now possible to go through the entire park and not see a bear at all. They have tried to keep them away from where people go. I have our family pictures of this trip and it is fun to see our excitement as we ran to the hourly eruption of Old Faithful. Actually, seeing something for real that we had learned about was exciting. I think my parents had already seen it on a vacation they took (without kids) in 1954. There were a lot of sights we did not see, but it was still a thrill being in the park. Our bear count was in excess of 20.

As Yellowstone and Grand Teton are basically adjacent it is easy to see both parks. The Grand Tetons and Jackson Lake were beautiful. Still are.

We had friends of my parents who lived in Denver. We spent a few days with them and had a good time seeing the sights around that area. That including picnicking on private property up in the mountains that had stocked lakes for fishing. I still didn't catch much. We made it right to the entrance of Rocky Mountain National Park in Estes Park, Colorado, but did not enter the park. We probably just didn't have the time.

On the way to the Grand Canyon we saw Mesa Verde, in southwest Colorado. That park has ancient Indian cliff dwellings.

We were there fairly early in the morning and the ruins were in the shadows of the cliffs. Again, we did not have time to get out to explore.

The Grand Canyon also did not have available camping spots, but they did open picnic areas for tent camping. It was a real thrill to see the canyon. The pictures have faded over the years, but it was a beautiful, clear day and we spent the morning there. We were pretty inexperienced in our picture taking and really did not consider sun location in setting up our shots. If you are on the west rim in the morning you are going to be taking pictures into the sun. In going through the Indian Reservation around Grand Canyon I recall my folks stopping to see how much the colorful Navaho rugs cost. Seems the cost was $6.00. Too much for my parents' budget. The little Indian kids would pull themselves up on our car asking for gum and candy. Other Indians were in full dress and would charge to take their picture.

In Utah that night we camped in Zion. I recall one of the pictures I had drawn in 5th grade of the "Great White Throne". And then there was Checkerboard Mesa. We got to see and photograph those sights and I felt Zion was a nice bonus for the trip. That night we all were in the tent and a storm came through. We all laid awake wondering if the tent would blow down. One of the metal fingers broke off that held up one corner of the tent to the frame. I think we awoke to another sunny day. Utah has several parks and Zion is the only one I have been to. Would love to go back to see the others.

Then 1961 we set off again for another two-week vacation. The majority of our time would be spent in Minnesota, where my dad grew up and in Ironwood, Michigan, where he was born. We saw a lot of sights in getting there and back. For example, we camped in Glacier. This was mid-July and we had ice in our dishpan when we got up in the morning. We were close to a lake and for some reason we kids felt we should try swimming. Way too cold. Around dinner time I left the camp area and went down a steep bank to the lake. I think I was washing the sand off my sandals. I heard a noise and looked up to see a bear running at me along the rocky beach followed by three cubs. The mother bear had garbage in her mouth. I froze. How do I get out of the way? Jump in the lake? Run up the bank? (It was steep and rocky). Then it was too late to do anything. The bear ran by me close enough to touch with the cubs close behind. Then I was able to get back to our camp. "Guess what just happened to me?"

I got the stomach flu the next day. Might have been the cold water of the lake or my dad's rubbery fried eggs that he made for my breakfast. So, I basically slept. However, when we got to Custer Battlefield, in eastern Montana, I had to get well quick or miss another sight I really wanted to see. I have now been there four times and learn more about that battle each time.

In North Dakota we stopped to see, what was then, Theodore Roosevelt National Monument near Medora. It is now the entrance to one of the Badlands National Park. Connie and I also returned here in 2011. There were no other National Parks between there and Michigan. However, on the way back we saw Mt. Rushmore, in the Black Hills. Still a favorite place of mine. Now that I live in Minnesota, we have made four trips to the Black Hills. There is more to see every time.

Just south of Wall, SD and east of the Black Hills is the Badlands of South Dakota. I'm not sure if it was an actual National Park in 1961. It was hot and we didn't have much time to stick around. Maybe a picture or two is all. I would not visit that park again until my son Dan and I visited in 2014 when I realized what the pictures were that we took in 1961.

As we continued our trip, we got fairly close to Devil's Tower in Wyoming. However, the only picture we have is from some distance. Again, I would get back to this National Monument in 2014.

For the second year in a row we visited Yellowstone. Again, we saw lots of bear including one that came right up to my dad's driver side window. While the picture is blurry it was still one of the trip highlights. Please note that all windows were closed as the bear approached the car. We also saw Old Faithful again. There is so much of Yellowstone we did not see on both the 1960 and 1961 trips that it was not until 2003 that Connie and I were able to see Yellowstone Falls and spend time watching the Bison in Hayden Valley.

We did another camping vacation in 1964 and I was 15 ½ and driving with my learners' permit. I drove some in all nine states we visited. We visited Custer again and then south to Denver. We went back by way of Salt Lake and then on to Yosemite, entering from the east over Tioga Pass, which was under construction and quite a scary drive. There was one car heading east that refused to drive on the right side of the road and forced us to the outside (cliff side). We camped in the park, but it would not be until the late 70's that I got to see much more of the park.

By this time I had seen about 13 of the parks plus some monuments. There was still half the country I had not seen, however, there are not near as many parks in the east.

We did go back to Crater Lake in 1966 on an Oregon vacation. We also spent time on the beautiful Oregon coast and visited Oregon Caves. Because of forest fires in the area we didn't even take pictures of the lake. The return trip was not memorable.

Starting in 1966 I always had summer jobs and did not take any more long trips with my folks. Maybe some weekend camping trips or an end-of-summer trip. These were usually in Washington or Oregon. It was quite a few years before I had a chance to visit any more parks.

In 1975 I had my first real one-week vacation. Connie and I camped in the new North Cascades National Park. I used my dad's camper and we had a very enjoyable stay that included some hiking and a ranger presentation. We had our husky Tasha with us. Sitting around the fire one evening the dog gave us very strong indications that she was uncomfortable and wanted to go to the camper. We finally killed the fires and climbed up into the camper. Within minutes we heard a terrible racket in the trash cans across the road from our campsite. By 1975 the trash cans were "bear proof", but that did not stop them from trying to get something. I swung open the back camper door and watched a very large bear meander by the truck and through our campsite. I bet that bear had a nightly route which went through our site. Our husky did not want to mess with that bear.

The following weekend we camped at Spirit Lake at Mt. St. Helens. While only part of a national forest I make mention of it because five years later this mountain blew away the top several thousand feet. The area where we camped no longer existed. It was nice to see the mountain before the eruption.

Connie and I moved to California in 1976 and Rick was born in 1978. That fall my folks came to visit with the camper and we all went to Yosemite and camped in the valley floor. We had our dog Erin and she and I slept in a tent so Connie and the baby (and my folks) had the camper. Erin did startle me by chasing after something in the night. She was tied and did reach the end of her rope. Just a raccoon that she chased under the truck. My mom and I hiked the trail to the base of Vernal Falls. I don't recall if it was this trip or another about two years later where I actually hiked to the top of Vernal Falls and then on to Nevada falls. A trip I would repeat with friends in 1985 when we hiked up the back side of Half Dome. In all we had several trips to Yosemite. However, we never made it to Kings Canyon or Death Valley which were several hundred miles south of us.

In the mid 80's we made a couple of trips to the Desolation Wilderness area of the Sierras. That was off US highway 50 and would be on the western side of Lake Tahoe. It was just a couple of hours from where we lived in Sacramento. Another place that was probably more of a state park, was Coloma where Sutter's Mill was located on the American River. The gold discovery site. I had the kids run their feet in the water and kick up the sand. We then looked for flakes of gold that might get stuck between their toes. I basically made this up, but the kids sure enjoyed "toeing" for gold.

I had one more memorable trip to Yosemite. Friends Don Murray and Jeff Smoot backpacked from the valley floor up past Vernal and Nevada falls and camped in a high meadow on the back side of Half Dome. Don wanted to live off the land but only managed to catch a small trout each night for dinner. Jeff and I shared our dehydrated dinners with him. We did have another bear encounter. In the "approved" camp areas the park provides metal lockers where you are supposed to put any food. These are bear proof. Then at night we would tie our packs up into trees that even if the bears climbed the packs would be hanging too far out on the limbs for them to reach. Sure enough, bears came into camp after dark and tried the locker and then tried to reach the packs by standing up tall. There was another group by us and one bear was able to stand up on its hind feet and reach a backpack and flip it over. All the contents fell to the ground. There was no food in the pack so I don't think any damage was done. What is funny is that I laid in my tent watching all this happen and was not worried about the bear bothering us. I think because there were three in our group plus other campers, we felt safety in numbers.

We moved to the Midwest in 1986 and by the fall of 1987 were in Carmel, Indiana where we would live until 2010. As mentioned, there are not as many parks in the east. We did have a Spring Break where we took the kids to Mammoth Cave, Kentucky. It was a nice tour, but these caves do not have the beautiful stalactites and stalagmites that other caves have. This was a former underground river bed and had some very large "rooms".

Another year we rented a cabin (house) above Gatlinburg, Tennessee. That is at the west entrance to Smokey Mountain National

Park. I would make several more trips to this area and visit the park on all those occasions. There are no fees to get into the park as the highway is one of the few routes to get over the Smokey's. There is a popular area where Appalachian Trail crosses the road. On a couple of occasions I hiked a portion of the trail just to say I did. If the area I hiked (maybe a mile) is any indication I would say that this would not be the easiest trail in the woods. On one of these trips the wild flowers were alive with butterflies. I got a few good pictures. So, you go to see the mountains and end up focusing on a very small part of the wildlife.

There are a lot of bears in this park and they are even on the edge of the town. I held an insurance training seminar in Gatlinburg in 2007 and it was fun taking people up into a part of the park that I had never seen before.

During all this time living in Indiana there were not any close parks to visit. I did see several of the more popular Civil War battlefields. Those included Gettysburg (twice), Antietam, Shiloh, and some smaller battle locations. Included in that would be Harpers Ferry which has its own pre-Civil War history. The battlefields are under the administrative jurisdiction of the National Park System, so they count in a way as to visiting.

Connie and I went to Hawaii in 2009 and spent about five days on the big Island. We took a day drive to Volcano's National Park. This has been an active area for years and part of the rim drive was closed the day we were there due to poisonous smoke coming out of the volcano. There are still areas where hot lava makes it to the ocean.

I'm not sure I can think of any additional parks we visited. Instead I have many repeats. Connie and I visited Yellowstone, Custer, and Mt. Rushmore again in 2003. In Yellowstone we stayed two nights in the Yellowstone Lake Lodge. Not as cool as the Old Faithful Inn. However, it was well situated for how we planned our travel around the park. We entered Yellowstone from the south and had lunch at the lodge at Grand Teton National Park.

In 2010 Connie and I moved to southwest Minnesota. Near us was a National Historical Monument called Pipestone. I knew nothing about it, until we took my sister and her husband there when they visited and found it very interesting. The Plains Indians found the red rock from which their peace pipes were carved. It is considered very sacred grounds and there are Indians there carving new pipes which can be purchased. Of interest my brother-in-law Dan pulled out his

National Park Pass and covered all our admissions. The next time I took company, probably one of my kids who were visiting, I bought my own pass. I am over 62 and for $10 I bought a lifetime pass for all National Parks and Monuments. It is good for up to three guests. What a deal. When Dan and I traveled to Devils Tower, Custer Battlefield and the Badlands National Park I was able to gain free admission for us which would have come to about $35. They have the system beat at Mt. Rushmore. The "park" is free. But they get you for about $12 to park. Oh well.

A few words about the trip Dan and I took in 2014. We stayed at a cabin in Custer State Park which is in the Black Hills and about 30 minutes from Mt. Rushmore. On the drive there we went right up to the base of Devil's Tower in Wyoming. Then after a night in Sheridan we spent several hours at the Custer Battlefield. It was my forth trip there, but the most meaningful. We took the time to drive along the top of the "ridge" and see how the entire battle played out. The actual location of "Custer's Last Stand" only accounted for about 15% of the entire regiment. The rest are spread out over a five-mile area.

After leaving the Black Hills we stopped in the Badlands National Park, which is just south of Wall SD. In addition to the unforgiving landscape we were fascinated by the big horn sheep. It was almost as if the park rangers put them close to the road for our enjoyment. As we got out of the car we saw more and more in the area.

I took my "around the country" Amtrak trip in the fall of 2015. I spent some time with two of my cousins on the Oregon coast and we found ourselves near Newport, Oregon at a lighthouse at Yaquina Head. The views from the point were very spectacular. We drove in only to find the admission was probably more than we expected for the time we were going to spend there. As we were planning on turning around the Ranger asked if any of us had our National Park pass. I DID! For some reason I put it in my wallet before I left on the trip. What a good investment for only $10. For as long as I can us it.

In 2011 Connie and I made it up to Medora, North Dakota. That is at the entrance of Theodore Roosevelt National Park. Remember I was there in 1961 and my folks stopped there on other trips they took. My dad really liked the history of the area so we drove all through the park. There are lots of bison, prairie dog villages and deer. Plus, some very interesting terrain. The "bad lands" is a very descriptive term. It is impossible to drive in a straight line anywhere in the park.

I have been very close to several other parks. I have been to the entrance of Rocky Mountain National Park. On my train trip I was close to Big Bend in Texas. I have flown over Canyonlands and Bryce Canyon and probably Arches in Utah. I would love to see Shenandoah in Virginia. Harpers Ferry is where the Shenandoah flows into the Potomac.

We have visited Mt. Vernon, Monticello, Colonial Williamsburg, and many other famous historical sites. So, my park quest is not over. I don't ever expect to see them all. The Everglades would be a neat visit and as my travels continue, I will expect to see more. I'll let you know how those turn out.

TELEVISION

Television is something we take totally for granted. Yet the television was introduced to the world when the baby boomers were children. When our parents were young there was no television and no one knew the difference. Most families had a radio and entertainment, major political events, or sporting events came into the house via radio. That is if you had electricity. My dad grew up with no electricity but heard radio at the home of people who did have power or through a crystal set. Crystal sets did not need a power source. They had a metal devise to clasp onto any metal object and listening was through headphones. Thus, the world would come in through the air.

Great events were broadcast on radio, like President Roosevelt's fireside chats or news of the war. There are many images of families sitting around the radio in silence to hear the news.

Many of the entertainers who we saw as kids on TV got their start on radio. Especially the singers and comedians.

Television may have become available much earlier had it not been for World War II. Consumer products were put on hold as the entire manufacturing and scientific resource efforts were put toward the war effort. My mother spent a lot of time in New York City as her father and sister lived there in the years just before the war. New York hosted a World's Fair in 1939 and 1940 and visitors could view themselves on television at the RCA exhibit. Mom saw herself on TV sometime during the fair. She probably did not see herself on TV again until we videotaped her with her grandkids over 40 years later.

I don't remember not having a TV. My parents got their first TV when I was about three years old in 1951. I remember watching TV in the evening, and kid's shows in the afternoon. But the set was often in the off position. Not sure why it was called a "set". But it was. The TV set was a piece of furniture. It came in a nice finished wooden cabinet, often with doors. Doors were closed when no one was watching it. The bottom was the speaker and the top was the picture tube. The TV image was the displayed electronically through the picture tube. There were two dials. The volume knob (also turned the TV on and off) and the channel selector. We had 12 numbers on the channel selector. As a child I could not figure out why there was not a channel one. Numbers went from 2-13. Most families near a big city got three basic channels (ABC, CBS, and NBC). If lucky you also got PBS and one or two independent channels.

There was not 24-hour TV. Networks were often off the air around mid-night and PBS and independents often were not on the air at all. Viewers were treated to the "test pattern" just before and after the station come on air. When they went off the air the national anthem played, and the test pattern would show for a while. You can see samples of test patterns on the internet. Usually it was an Indian chief and focusing lines that allowed the adjusting of the settings of the TV.

Early TV's were not very reliable. They were expensive based on what incomes were in the 50's. Several things could go wrong which usually meant an evening production of testing tubes. When you took off the back panel of the TV you were presented with a maze of circuits and glowing tubes. With the TV on dad would remove a tube to determine what was affected. It could be the sound, or vertical hold, or horizontal hold, or picture sharpness, etc. Fact is I have no idea what all the tubes were for. However, miniature circuitry had not been invented yet nor transistors which minimized many of the circuit components.

We could have called a TV repairman, but that was expensive. The first attempt was to try to fix it yourself. Often dad would pull a few tubes (being careful not to mix them up) and take them to the drug store where they had "tube tester" machines. Those machines would tell if the tube was still good or not and if lucky, we would find the bad tube on the first try. If not, dad came home, reinserted the tubes and took out a few more. There were probably only 7 or 8, but it seemed like more. When we found a bad tube you could buy a replacement and might be back in business if it worked right. Sometimes this production took several evenings, and we would miss our favorite shows.

There was not another TV to watch in the house, so you just found something else to do.

The TV signal came from tall TV towers (hundreds of feet high). The tower on the top of the Empire State building in New York City broadcast the local New York channels. Individual sets did a poor job of picking up the signal, even if in direct sight of the towers (as ours was in Seattle). Most houses had an antenna attached to their chimney with a cable running down the side of the house, through the walls and into the back of the TV. If you moved the TV, you had to move the cable. We were very fancy in that our antenna could be rotated from a motor so we could shift the angle of the antenna to better pick up the independent stations that were not in Seattle.

Other sets had "rabbit ears" which you still see today on some High Definition sets that are not hooked up to cable or satellite. It seemed the TV would lose its prime viewing angle and it could be a group effort to try to find the best position of the antenna for viewing.

We sometimes successfully brought in stations from some distance. Late at night we sometimes could bring in the station from Victoria, British Columbia or Bellingham, Washington. The later was about 90 miles to the north. It didn't matter what was on, we would watch the "snowy" picture just because we could.

If we missed a show, we missed the show. The only chance in seeing a favorite episode of a missed show was to wait for summer reruns. Many of the prime time shows used the summer months to rebroadcast episodes. Even if we had seen them before we would watch reruns.

One's "favorite" shows were what your parents watched. They seemed to always have a priority in what played on the set. Therefore, I never watched some famous shows like Andy Griffin because my dad had a show to watch that he liked. That meant that we watched all the westerns, and cop shows. There were a lot of westerns. "Gunsmoke", "Cheyenne", "Wagon Train", "Maverick", "Sugarfoot", "The Virginian", and the list goes on. Cop and detective shows like the "Untouchables", or "Dragnet" were popular for years. When I was in high school we finally got a "portable" second set. That was a smaller set and we could watch it in our basement "rec room" using built in rabbit years. In high school I would watch "Man from Uncle" or "Lost in Space" while my dad watched his shows.

Most singers and entertainers had their own variety shows or appeared as guests on these shows. Mom could watch Perry Como or Andy Williams each week and see many famous guests. Those shows would be where we might see Frank Sinatra or Sammy Davis Jr. Lucy, Burns and Allen, and Jack Benny carried their radio success to television and were my favorites. The "sit coms" are the only type of TV show that have survived for today's viewers. Cop shows are also still popular. Gone are the variety shows (Ed Sullivan) and westerns.

Most of kid programming was locally produced. Growing up in the 50's and early 60's the Seattle stations had Captain Puget, Stan Boreson, JP Patches, Brakeman Bill, Wanda Wanda, and probably a few other shows for kids. They were usually on in the early morning or after school in the afternoon. JP Patches was on both times. The production sets were right in the local studio. Captain Puget was set below decks of a small sail boat. JP Patches had a shack at the town dump, and Stan had his "Club House" with his trusted companion No-Mo (a basset hound) and accordion. All the shows had skits and played cartoons. I think Stan also played some of the Little Rascals. Cub Scout or Girl Scout groups often were on these shows live and we usually knew when a friend was going to be on. My brother John was on JP Patches. During the Seattle World's Fair of 1962, the local NBC affiliate (KING) did all their local programming from the fair grounds. We could watch the news being broadcast live and I had a chance to be one of the kids standing on the set during the Stan Boreson show. Of course, no one at home saw me. I had no way of telling them I was going to be on. Funny that my mom and I both had TV debuts at a World's Fair just 22 years apart.

Oh, and I need to mention. All the viewing of the 50's and most of the 60's was in black and white. Shows like Disney or Bonanza broadcast in color, but the early color sets were very expensive and not reliable. Many families waited for the prices to drop and for more shows to be broadcast. Then your existing set had to break. Dad was not going out to buy a color set as long as we had a perfectly good black and white set.

While I saw color programming at friends' houses (Star Trek on Fridays after HS basketball), it was not until I went to college, where the dorm TV was a large color set, that I saw it on a regular basis.

Speaking of college. No one took their own TV's to school. For all the reasons already mentioned. Size of sets, expense and no room to place them. Thus, the TV lounge was the real social location of a dormitory. We might have had seating for 20 students yet might crowd in 50 for a popular show or sporting event. By college "Star Trek" continued and shows like "The Smothers Brothers Comedy Hour" filled the room with viewers.

The first sporting events I remember watching was the 1959 World Series (Dodgers and White Sox) followed the next year by the 1960 Olympics. The Winter Olympics that year were from Squaw Valley in California. It seems that ABC's Wide World of Sports had the market cornered and we could watch replays of many of the week's events on their Saturday afternoon show. I don't recall that much live coverage during the week. The 1960 Summer Olympics were in Rome and prior to Satellite they had to fly film to New York every day to have something make the late news. Again, we could catch up on Saturdays. There was one college football game on TV each Saturday. Keith Jackson was the Seattle ABC (KOMO) sports guy and left to do the College Game of the Week. Most World Series games were played during the day and if the games were on the East Coast (as was often the case with the Yankees playing most years), we had morning World Series times in Seattle. I was home for lunch in the 6th grade when Bill Mazeroski hit the home run for Pittsburgh to beat the Yankees in game 7 of the 1960 series. I hurried back to school (one block) to be the first to tell all my class mates who had not gone home for lunch.

I don't recall watching any TV at school until the 6th grade. A couple of things happened in early 1961 that brought out the only set the school had. First was the January 20, inaugural of President Kennedy. He would be sworn in at 9:00 Pacific Time and I had been watching at home not wanting to go to school and miss such an historic event. When I got to school I was surprised that the 6th graders got to go the auditorium to watch the inaugural on the school TV. How cool, we got to watch TV at school. Then in May, Alan Sheppard was the first American launched into space. The flight was a short sub-orbital flight and was in fact over before we got to school, but Mr. Bogardus had the TV in his Science class and we watched late morning coverage of the event. I became a fan of the space program from that moment. Eventually getting up very early in Seattle to watch later launches live.

By the time my kids were in high school every class room had a color TV, their morning announcements were from the school TV studio (parents could watch at home on the "local access station"). A couple boys I knew were busted when they skipped school to see the Cubs opener in Chicago only to be seen by their class as the teacher had the game on at school. A true Ferris Bueller event. By this writing the TV's were out of the classrooms being replaced by "smart boards". Those could show shows directly from a computer or the internet.

Video recording did not become reasonable priced for families until the mid-80's. Then the cameras were big (they had to hold the VCR tape) and expensive. We often reused tapes wiping out cherished family memories. But not to worry. We still have hours of boys' baseball games, hockey games, Christmas mornings and orchestra recitals. Some are very painful to watch in their entirety years later. Ah, but new technology. I can burn these tapes onto a DVD and then edit out the boring stuff.

When we got married in 1973 my dad gave us a color set for a wedding present. It was a 19-inch Sanyo and at the time had very good color. If I recall the cost was $400. In current dollars that is more than a new flat screen today.

Now all of my kids took TV's away to college. They all had their own TV in their rooms at home and would watch any one of hundreds of channels. There are no longer TV rooms in college dorms thus ending a great social event allowing you to get to know most of the people living in your dorm. Families may still watch TV together, but even if the kids are watching the same program they may do so from their own room or space.

RADIO

Even with the invention of TV, radio was still a big part of our life growing up. Radio is where we first heard Elvis, listened to baseball games, tried to pick up stations from around the country, and argued over what station to listen to when riding in the car.

Radio was pretty much only AM. Even if someone had a nice console (another "set" hidden in a piece of furniture) which had FM stations they were reserved for classical type formats that did not play well on regular AM. About the time I was in college was when FM stations started playing album sides of Dylan and other popular artists of the 60's.

The biggest change for radio, and probably as radical as the invention of MP3 players, was the transistor radio. Remember tubes? Well large radio sets had them too. The transistors replaced the tubes allowing for miniaturization. While not as small as my iPod, the transistor was pretty compact and made listening to music or games something you do outside of your home or car. I would go to sleep at night listening to ball games or my favorite music station. But the biggest thing I remember was we sometimes got permission to have our radio at school during the day-time World Series games or for space shots. Teachers were generally tolerant and we usually asked permission the day before. We had to keep the sound down or use an ear piece. Or, one boy (girls did not care) would be allowed to listen and give the rest of the class updates with a score change.

Even in high school I remember listening to America's first spacewalk (Ed White) while in study hall.

Many kids learned radio "hobbies" from their parents. One was to listen late at night to see how many stations you could pick up from around the country. The AM signal could travel over 1000 miles if there was not another station using the same frequency that was closer. From Seattle I could easily pick up KGO in San Francisco, and stations if Albuquerque 770, Des Moines, Chicago, Los Angeles, and many others. My dad bought me a short-wave radio which picked up many more frequencies. At night I could find Japan (at least the music was Japanese) London and the Voice of America. When heavy weight fights were on there was usually a black out for normal TV and radio. However Armed Forces Radio often did round-by-round reviews for the military stationed all over the world. So, my short-wave radio became popular in listening to some sporting events.

I mentioned Crystal sets. They did not require electricity. As a kid you could still buy kits and make your own radio. I had a very inexpensive set that I just needed to attach with a clip to anything metal. I used the lampshade frame from the lamp on my nightstand. There was no speaker, so I used an ear piece. I could slip a small rod up and down to bring in different frequencies. My favorite station to find was KGO in San Francisco. There I listened to my first experience with a "talk radio" (Ira Blue?), and radio mysteries that broadcast like "Tales from Scotland Yard". They usually started by a couple of agents going through their collection of case evidence and something leading to a story about the case, which was acted out with sound effects and all. Something my parents must have been very used to prior to television, but in a few short years there was not much radio drama left on the air.

A "major appliance" that I took to college with me was a clock radio. That is one invention that has evolved, but still serves the same purpose many years later – to wake someone up with music instead of an annoying alarm.

Now days we occasionally have the need to just listen to a radio. For example, the Indy 500 is not broadcast live on TV in the Indianapolis area. They want you to go to the race. Also, the race is shown in its entirety in the evening so those who attended the race can see the television perspective. In the years we did not go to the race it was often a hassle finding a simple radio that we could listen to the race on. It usually meant bringing in someone's clock radio.

Radio stations now have much of their programming produced by a centralized corporation and have lost the local flair. I have not heard "lost cow" reports for many years while listening to the radio. In fact, satellite radio has totally taken any local news or flavor out of communications. All for the better?

WHERE HAVE ALL THE CABOOSES GONE?

Trains have always fascinated kids. At least boys. I still like to watch trains go by and am occasionally delayed as a long, slow train blocks my path. The only thing that I see different today from the trains of my youth is that trains no longer have a caboose. I had really never thought about the reason for the absence of cabooses. It was just something I noticed.

Trains were part of the American westward expansion. They tied the country together and allowed travel that previously had been done by wagon at the rate of 15 miles a day. Trains could cover 100's of miles a day and bring products and goods to those who had moved west. Somehow, even as a kid one sensed the history, glamor, and appeal of the train. Most interesting to kids were the old steam locomotives. The smoke and noise and the whistle were amazing. Who could not find trains fascinating? I rode on an old train pulled by a steam locomotive when I was nine years old. Probably the summer of 1958. I rode with my mom from Seattle to Snoqualmie Falls and back. To this day I know we "cheated". To pull the grade of the Cascade foothills we had a diesel locomotive pushing us. The ride was very fun. For the first time in my life I was able to look out the open windows and see the front of the train clearly as we made curves. You never had that feeling in a car. And the rest room. Flush the toilet and you could see the rail ties that the train passed over. Now that was weird. I'm sure I went running back to my mom telling her what I had discovered.

In that ride the rail lines ran parallel to US Hwy 10 heading east out of Seattle. I noticed that a convertible was matching our speed and mounted over the seats was a tripod with a Hollywood type movie camera set up. A man was filming us as his driver kept pace. Of course, I felt waving was appropriate, but every time I waved I could tell the cinematographer was upset and threw his arms up in an irritated motion. Finally, my mom saw what I was doing and told me to stop waving. The man was trying to catch us on film which did not entail kids waving at the camera. To this day I wonder where that film ended up. Hope I did not ruin too much footage. Also, I seem to remember the police having the car pulled over once. Wonder why?

Ever wonder how trains turn around? I still do. The train reached Snoqualmie Falls and the steam engine uncoupled and took off. Half hour later it showed up heading back down the mountain. My mom could not explain exactly how they did that.

Her background had been a life of trains. Their family, living in Philadelphia, never had a car. In fact, neither she nor her siblings ever drove. My grandfather worked for the railroad and trains took them anywhere they needed to go. When my mom got older, she often took the train to New York City to visit her dad and sister, who had moved there after high school. In 1946 mom was able to get a job transfer to Seattle, where her now married sister lived. She packed up a trunk of all her worldly possessions and took the train to Seattle. That was as far from Philadelphia as she could get. And she never returned.

As a kid many of my friends had electric trains. These were toys that allowed hours of fun. Adding track to make the route longer, adding cars, like the barrel unloader, and automatically uncoupling and hooking back up the cars could fill up a day. My set basically did a figure 8, but some of my friends had dads who had constructed big sets that took up half of the basement. The miniature HO gage had come out allowing very detailed sets with paper mache mountains and little towns. A real treat would be to be allowed to operate a train. These sets were totally hands-off when a dad was not around. As tempting as they were my friends knew that to break something on their dad's set was about the worse thing a kid could do.

My set was a Lionel. My friend Louie had an American Flyer. He had more realistic looking track (two rails) whereas Lionel had a center rail that supplied power to the rails and thus the locomotive. While it did not look totally realistic, Lionel was easier to add extensions. The American Flyer Company folded at some point leaving only Lionel. You can still buy track, cars, and towns for Lionel Trains today. I still have my set but would have to replace the transformer (large scale power adapter with controls).

As a boy of six or seven my dad took me to Woodland Park in Seattle one day after he got home from work. I knew Woodland Park as the location of the zoo. But that day we did not go to the zoo. Instead we watched a work crew transfer a full-size steam locomotive from a large heavy-duty truck to rails that had been set up to display the train. Even as a young kid I was amazed at how the men were able to move such a heavy object as a locomotive. I got very nervous that it would tip or fall and finally persuaded my dad to take me home. Dad loved to watch things like that. You can find the history of that locomotive on the internet, but the dates vary as to when it was brought in and eventually removed.

Our family was always going places where trains blocked our route. You could not drive in or out of West Seattle without going over busy rail lines on Harbor Island. Lots of the ocean-going fright was off-loaded in Seattle and trains blocked traffic on a regular basis. The roadway is now elevated. That is the case in most places around the country. Especially around the big cities. The trains are still there, but most modern highways are not bothered by them. In the summer of 1964, we were on a family vacation and were heading south through Wyoming. We got an early start and were going to have breakfast in Laramie. We would be in Denver later in the day. My dad loved the wide-open road. On this particular morning we were passed by a freight train. My dad decided to find out how fast the train was moving. He reached 95 before finally backing off. We never did really reach the speed of the train. That was probably the fastest I had gone at that point in my life.

As kids we liked the diversion of being held up by a train. Counting the cars became a regular event. We always speculated what was in all those box cars. Where were they going? Where had they come from? Was it a good job to run the trains? The one thrill we all got as kids was waving at the engineer and as the train finally came to its end there was always someone with their arm out the window of the caboose just waiting to wave to us. It seemed that was their only purpose. Even though my grandfather had worked for the railroad, my mom really could never exactly tell us what they did in the caboose. We guessed it was sleeping quarters for the engineers and a place to eat. How the engineer got all the way to the back then brought up another mystery and problem to solve.

In the early 70's my future wife and I were traveling with a friend (Sue) from Oregon back to Seattle on Interstate 5. About 90 south of Seattle Sue pointed to a train we were overtaking. Something about it was very strange. Cars were derailing as we watched. It almost seemed in slow motion as every car folded the opposite direction as the one in front of it in an accordion type position. We really did not hear any noise. I was driving a pickup truck and had a camera in the back. By the time we got safely stopped about 20 cars had derailed and a cloud of dust filled the air. The locomotive was already backing up toward the wreckage. The cargo was new cars. The next day a very small article in the Seattle paper mentioned the accident. A broken rail was to blame.

I always enjoy my experiences with trains. Before I had my own car in college, I could ride the 90 miles home on weekends via train. It probably cost all of three dollars and it was a relaxing way to sit back, do some reading, and watch scenery that was usually not seen on the interstate. I would get in on a Friday afternoon about the time my dad would be driving home from work, so it usually worked out well for him to pick me up.

By 1976 I worked in San Francisco for two years and lived in the east bay. BART (Bay Area Rapid Transit) was my way into work. While just a commuter train I joined the millions of Americans around big cities who rode trains to work. Then when our kids were older we could take excursions on Amtrak into down town Los Angeles. A fun family outing just a few years ago was to take the train from suburban New Jersey into New York's Grand Central Station.

Living in Sacramento we were treated to a fabulous railroad museum. Sacramento is an inland city that is at sea level and just to the east is the start of the Sierra Nevada foothills. Drive just 20 miles east and the elevation is at 1000 feet. Therefore, the trains that went out of Sacramento were the most powerful locomotives built anywhere. One combination engine and tender car displayed in the Railroad Museum weighs close to 1 million pounds. My wife's father was living in Europe when we lived in Sacramento. Every summer he would spend a week with us. He loved the railroad museum. After high school (1934) and before joining the army, just before World War II, Jack worked for the railroad in Los Angeles. His dad had been a railroad worker and looked to his son to having a career with the railroad. While touring the museum he became an unofficial tour guide demonstrating how he would grease the wheels and axles of the big locomotives before they headed to points east out of Los Angeles, where he lived. My kids were there, but probably did not appreciate the lesson they were getting from someone with firsthand experience. Jack had actually worked with the last of the locomotives in the 1930's. The museum even had a roundhouse. We could see how trains could be turned around.

Another train experience came from have an excursion on a Dinner Train out of Lewistown, Montana. This train went across the Montana prairie and riders got a meal and the excitement of being "held up" by robbers on horseback.

Now I live in a small Minnesota town and trains come through town just two blocks from my house. The whistle will wake me up at night, but I really don't mind. Trains bring back all the old childhood memories. Before I retired my office looked out on tracks where one large freight train an hour went by, in either direction. Sometimes there were 100 cars of coal (I am guilty to still counting the cars) or tanker cars full of corn syrup from the big corn plant in Marshall. Many of the trains have multiple diesel locomotives pulling them. Now after all these years trains are still trains but we don't have to stop for them as often as the past. Except in rural areas roads have been built over, under and around major rail routes. However, there is still the question that replaced the many train questions we all had as kids. None of the trains today ever have a caboose. Where did all the cabooses go?

I guess they are no longer needed. Railroads have many automatic track switching features now and crews can be replaced or rotated at scheduled stopping points. They don't need to go to the back of the train to rest. Likewise, they don't need to sit up high and wave to all the people sitting in their cars waiting for train to pass, as they count the cars.

Finally, I took my 10,000 mile rail trip in 2015. The narrative of that adventure can be found elsewhere in this book. However, the only cabooses I saw were sitting on deserted side rails. No longer being used and perhaps waiting for a train buff to purchase and restore.

I DON'T WANT A PICKLE

This dissertation has nothing to do with the Arlo Guthrie song with the same title. He just wanted to ride his motorcycle. I just don't want a pickle.

When I was young, I didn't like anything I had never eaten before. "I don't like it" was a normal statement. So, what was I afraid of? I have no idea, but I can remember trying many common foods for the first time. We were a meat and potatoes family. No rice, no pizza, no salads, no special sauces, and by my personal choice virtually no condiments. The basic ingredients of a hamburger were left off until I was in my 20's. I ate my hamburgers "plain". That is just a bun and meat.

I was probably in junior high school the first time I tried lettuce. I had to be convinced it really had no taste so it would be okay. Lettuce was fine after that. I did like ketchup with French Fries. At some point I probably got brave and added that to a burger. I'm not sure when cheese came into play. I didn't like most cheeses and never just ate a hunk of cheese. I did not voluntarily eat a tomato until after I was married. That was only to save face. My wife's grandfather had a garden in which he grew "beef steak" tomatoes. We visited him in 1976 and the tomatoes were offered as a "treat". Just add salt and eat with a knife and fork. I didn't choke or gag so after that I could eat a tomato. I never have liked mustard. There are some gourmet blends that I will try, but just basic yellow mustard, no thanks.

There's more. I didn't like any type of onions. My mom liked to season many foods with onions. Cut up very small. I always finished a meal with a small pile of onions on the side of my plate. Especially challenging was her spaghetti. She made it as a casserole, and it had lots of onions. I could find most of the little bits and remove them.

My dad's older sister was a very good cook and I recall her making breakfast potatoes and the smell of the onions cooking was so heavy in the air I had to leave the room. However, I loved the potatoes and her onions were cut larger than my mom's so I could pick them out and push them to the side of my plate. In later years I learned to like cooked onions and will even include them in things I make. But, not the same for raw onions. The smell of raw onions overwhelms anything they are around so they would not make it to a burger. I could never figure out mayo. Why add to a burger? I use mayo to mix tuna or in lieu of butter on a sandwich, but I think it just makes a burger messier.

That leaves pickles. Fast food places cut them up and bury them in a burger. First thing I must do is fish them out. My wife gets them, so they do not go to waste. I like Burger King Whoppers as you can easily include (or not) the condiments you want. Wendy's is the same way. So, my burger now might include cheese, lettuce, tomato, and ketchup. That's it. When doing road trips, we often eat while driving to save time. I have learned that the McDonalds Double Cheeseburger is a good item as it does not drip sauce. It is easy to hold and eat, once the pickles have been removed. They usually just put in two slices and there are times that I will bite into one. It's not the end of the world, but the balance of the pickle is removed and discarded.

All that being said I want to reflect on the fact that many restaurants like to give you a pickle wedge with any sandwich you order for lunch. Some of these are quite big. I never have understood the purpose of this addition to the meal. Is it done to make a better meal presentation? Are they just messing with me? Do I have to pay for this? My meal cost is not reduced if I tell the server "no pickle please". Most restaurant burgers are served with the condiments on the side. I like that as I can include the couple I like. Lettuce and tomato. I can leave the pickle for my wife and I try to get the onion as far as possible from my plate so as not to pollute my sense of smell.

I have to wonder how many pickles I have left uneaten in my lifetime. Especially the wedges. Hundreds. Maybe into the thousands.

What in the heck is a pickle anyway? It is a cucumber (which I can eat on salads) that is soaked in a vinegar brine to ferment into a pickle. When bottled it can last years. The process has been around for hundreds of years and it was a food source that could travel on sailing ships and with army's and would not spoil. A good source of something. Napoleon liked pickles. More power to him. Somehow the pickle has become part of our diet. Not as a necessity, but by choice. Or, because some kind of pickle lobby has continued to convince restaurants to service wedges with sandwiches.

I don't know where to begin in guessing the amount of pickles that I have wasted in my life. According to the internet (it must be right) the average American eats 8 pounds of pickles a year. That would mean that I have not eaten 400 pounds of pickles in my adult life. Since the slices get passed to my wife I will focus on the wedges. Those are cucumbers about six inches long that are quartered lengthwise. Since I traveled a lot in my work and ate out a lot, I probably averaged one of these a week for years. Let's do the math. I will not start counting until I was 20. Prior to that I probably didn't eat lunch out that often. I have over 40+ years of ignoring my pickle wedge. At one a week that would be about 2300 pickle wedges. If made whole that would be almost 600 cucumbers. So how many pickles (cucumbers) in a one jar? Six? That is 100 jars. How many jars in a case? 12? That is 8 to 9 cases of pickles that I have been served to me that I did not eat. This will continue as long as I eat lunches out. Boy we waste a lot of food in this country.

I don't want those pickles. I don't want any pickles. I can only think of a couple of times where I told the server in advance to hold the pickle. The wedges usually don't get eaten by my wife as she usually has her own.

I am not against anyone else eating pickles. I don't mean to lobby to discontinue the serving of pickles. I would guess that most people do eat them. I just don't want them. I feel guilty in not eating everything put on my plate. Yet the plate goes back to the kitchen with the pickle wedge still there. Do they all end up in the trash? Do they just get passed along to the next order? What does the restaurant pay for them? How much of our meal price includes the cost of a pickle wedge?

I have picked on the pickle. I could go after parsley, or bread, or other things that restaurants bring with your meal that end up not being consumed. I just think the pickle is the most obvious. When served as a wedge it can be the largest single item that we are served that was not actually ordered. I have never heard anyone ask for a second pickle or to include two in their order. In fact, I have gotten so used to ignoring the pickle that I am sure most of the time I don't even acknowledge its presence. I just move it out of the way.

Like I said, "I don't want a pickle."

CORRESPONDENCE

Communications has seen one of the most marvelous advancements in technology in the life of the baby boomers. To the point that the talking part of communications is not even important anymore when we can text and email. My aunt (born in 1919), complained that no one wrote anymore. She was referring to the lack of correspondence to her from me or my kids. "Sara, you just need a computer and we can "talk" every day." Of course, she did not get it and would never have considered getting a computer when a hand-written note or letter worked perfectly well. Until there was no one left of her generation to write to her.

We always had a phone. Basic phone service was fairly expensive and few of our friends and relatives could afford "long distance" calls. Long distance was anything outside of your geographic area. In Seattle that probably meant King County. Since the county was so big I'm not sure that all distant county calls were free. My parents might make one long distance a month and made sure they watched their minutes. When I moved away and talked to my parents, or Aunt Sara, on the phone you had to worry about a long call. Say what you had to say, thank them for calling and say bye. You kept calls short.

When I was in college our dorms made the big transition from a pay phone in each stairwell to putting phones in each room. It was not uncommon for kids to be begging for money to pay their phone bill. The access of a phone in the room meant they could talk to all their friends at home. Then they got their bill. $85 was one amount that I remember one girl having to come up with. She could not tell her parents. After all they had warned her about long distance bills. After I graduated and was engaged my future wife was still a student back at

44

school. I remember some $15.00 calls which would be like $50 today. Just for one call.

There was only one Phone Company. Simply called "the phone company". Until the government broke up Bell Telephone there was no competition. After all they had put the infrastructure in place and a competitor would have meant duplicating all of that. Even when it did break up it was more on a regional basis than multiple carriers at the local level.

Phone service in the 50's was slowing growing. Our number in Seattle was AValon 2494. When you dialed (no push buttons yet), you would dial AV 2494. Soon by the late 50's the phone company was running out of numbers, so they added the 7th digit. Area codes came a little later. When we changed to seven numbers our prefix changed. (Oh my God!). So, we were then WEst 5-2494. Now we would say 935-2494, but my mom always said West. (For West Seattle). My parents had that number until they died in 2005. We had one old phone which sat on the kitchen counter. We kept the kitchen stool next to the phone so my dad could sit if he was talking.

At first, we had a party line. That was very common in the country where my cousins had a 4-party line. Either the rings were a different pattern, or the phone would only ring at the correct residence. When you picked up the phone and heard another party already talking you were supposed to quickly hang up and try later. If it was an emergency you could politely ask if you could make a call. Usually you knew the other people on the party line. I don't think my mom ever met the other party on our phone, but she had talked to them and knew they lived over on the "other hill." At some point my parents felt they could afford a single party line and we never had to share a line again.

Some other things I remember about old phone service was if my mom wanted to talk to her mother in Philadelphia or her sister in San Francisco, she would dial "0" for the operator and they would place the call. You could ask that you only wanted to talk to a certain party. If that person was not available the operator would terminate the call and we would not be charged for the call.

If you wanted an extra phone it would cost you. My dad wanted a phone in the basement where he had his work bench. It would be hard for him to get upstairs to the kitchen when he heard the phone ring. But my dad was cheap and didn't want to pay for an extra phone, (the phone company actually owned all the phones). Someone he knew gave him an extra phone (a very old outdated model) that he hooked up in our basement. With that he could pick up calls in the basement and two people could listen in on a call at the same time. Problem was that phone also rang and in ringing it used power. Someone at the phone company could tell multiple phones were ringing and one night my dad got a call telling him he would have to disconnect that extra line or pay for two lines. My dad unhooked it. Busted by the Phone Company.

Sometime in the late 50's or early 60's the phone company added area codes. Those extra three digits, that we still use today, allowed us to call directly to any phone in the country and we no longer needed the operator to place calls to my grandmother in Philadelphia. The 10-digit extensions we now use have been around now for about 60 years or so. Since then the "1" was added for long distance and "800" numbers added so that the number called payed for the call.

After I started working for Continental Insurance in 1975, I would come home and comment on the fact that I got to call Alaska or New York. That was cool as it was company money. We always had to ask about the weather before we got down to business. I remember seeing our office phone bills and the typical Alaska call would be about $6.00. So, we had a Telex. You say "what?" We would write out a message and give it to our Telex operator. She typed the message on a tape. After placing the tape in the Telex unit, the number was called to another machine at our calling location. The message would be completed in less than a minute. Those calls cost about $2.50. No talk about the weather.

When away from home your only choice was the pay phone to call home. As kids we always carried a couple of dimes. If we went to the movies and needed to be picked up, etc. we just made a quick call home. You never talked long on a pay phone as if you did the operator cut in requesting more coins. If you were making a long distance call you would dial "0" and tell the operator where you were calling. She (always a she) would then tell you how much for the first three minutes. To save a dime our parents would work out a deal where we would call and listen for two rings and then hang up. We got our dime back and our parents knew it was time to come pick us up.

I must add a comment here. My dad always was looking for angles to save a nickel or a dime. We did our grocery shopping on Saturday mornings. My dad avoided the store parking lot as he felt other drivers were careless in hitting his car with their car door. (Many were careless). So, he parked on the street. Problem was there were meters and parking cost 5 cents, probably for an hour. We would drop off mom and dad would circle the block until he found a spot with some time left on the meter. One usually opened up fairly quickly. I would go in the store to help my mom finish her shopping and to tell her where we parked. My dad sat in the car so if the meter expired and the "meter reader" came by he could move and avoid paying the nickel. True story.

When people traveled or went away you would probably not talk to them again until you saw them again. That could be a couple of weeks or maybe even years. When I was in college my family took a three-week vacation one year and I stayed home as I had a summer job. About two weeks into their trip a post card might arrive. Otherwise we didn't talk until they got back home. The summer I graduated I went to Montreal from Seattle to visit the World's Fair. Expo 67. I was gone from Monday to Friday. There was never anything in our plan to call to check in. I imagined my great grandfather leaving Sweden in the 1890's and not seeing his wife and kids that were left behind for a couple of years. While they wrote the mail had to take weeks. I thought we had advanced as at least travel did not take as long. We just got by without talking to people.

Science Fiction writers imagined the cell phone, of sorts. Dick Tracy, in comics, used a two-way wrist radio. When the first cellular phone came out, they were very big and the joke was how someone could wear that on their wrist.

Our parents never changed their communication habits. My mom wrote letters giving me the latest news and what was going on. As we lived in California when our children were small we sent a lot of pictures via the mail to grandparents. My wife's folks lived in Germany. They got pictures too.

In 1976 I was transferred, and my wife and I moved to San Francisco. Starting about that time my mom called every Saturday evening. They had no kids left at home and the long-distance rates must have dropped. My dad had paid off the house in 1969 so they had a few extra dollars to splurge. For the next 30 years I got a Saturday night phone call. We changed the calling times over the years. In summer we always were out at boy's ball game and she might call later. We lived in the Eastern Time zone and Seattle was Pacific Time, so she had to keep track of the time difference.

My parents never had a cell phone and it was not until the late 90's when they switched out their dial phones (by that time they had a legal phone in the basement) and had pushbutton. My mom would watch me unplug the phone ("what are you doing"!!??) and plug in my laptop so I could check email. She would just shake her head. I remember, about that same time, our daughter was in a marching band competition at the University of Toledo, in Ohio. We were walking through campus and I realized my mom would call our home number and we would not be there. So, I called her on my cell phone. She still thought it was amazing that we could call her anywhere in the country and have a connection that was better than a local call.

However, my folks seldom called me on my cell phone. For one reason no one programmed it into her limited speed dial directory. Secondly, she felt she was bothering me. One time on a visit with my folks in Seattle I left to run an errand and was probably gone for less than an hour. When I got back my mom proceeded to tell me about the excitement they had right after I left. My dad had fallen and while he was okay, she could not get him up. So, they called the fire department who came in and got him into his chair and left. (It had not been their first or last visit to do that). I asked my mom when it happened, and she said I had been pulling out of the driveway. When I asked her why she had not called me she said she didn't want to bother me. Oh well.

Of course, I have a cell phone and have no problem texting. My employees usually text me to say they are going to be late, etc. I admit it is easier and quicker than taking a phone call for the same situation. I probably don't begin to use my phone for all the capability it has. I don't feel a need to access the internet via my phone. I'm not against anyone else doing it; I just don't personally feel I have a need. While the technological advances are tremendous in one generation, I find I sometimes take the same attitude my parents did. "Why bother."

By 2010 we finally did away with our "house phone". My cell is now my only number, and no one seems to have an issue with that. Same for all my kids. I have traveled all over the US and have called friends from the beach in Hawaii or almost out of light of land off Key West. No extra charges. Just part of our monthly service. I recall one of my boys averaging close to 80 text messages a day. I'm nowhere close to that number.

I wish my aunt was still around so I could complain that "no one talks to each other anymore." They write! Some irony in that. Now Aunt Sara would not approve of the lack of cursive writing skills and the short cryptic nature of notes, but quite frankly, I am fine with no more cursive. I was terrible at it.

THE LAST TIME

Much of what we do in life is repetitive. Our daily routine can stay the same for years. We might have a slightly different routine for school or work days than the weekend, but we are consistent in those routines. There is no sentiment attached to most of our daily chores, they are just things we do. If we give up one and replace with another it is usually no big deal. I don't get emotionally attached to a car or a lawn mower. They are just things I use and when I need a new one, I replace them. Even the memory of the first drive in a new car has faded as I have had a lot of new cars.

That being said there are many things is life that we will do for the last time. Many are things that we anticipate. The last day of school. The sad occasion of saying good bye to a dog that is old and dying. There can be emotional feelings in some of these last things. Compare the last day of school to the last day of summer vacation. Good and sad emotions. I bet I was not the only one who was teary eyed when on my last day of school ever the seniors were invited to the front hall way of the school to sing the school song one last time as a student. "West Side High, my alma mater".

At this writing I am 50 years since my high school graduation. For 13 school years I would see some of my friends every day. Those I didn't meet until high school maybe had a 3- or 4-year friendship. Then we graduate…. 50 years later you are hoping some of these old friends show up at the class reunion. You hope most are still alive. We all went off to different lives. While we knew the last day of school was a major transition in life, I don't think we realized that it would mean not seeing friends ever again.

There are fond memories of first kisses, but maybe not so much of last kisses. You may not have known at the time that it was a "last kiss". As relationships evolve and end, we may not even think about things happening for the last time.

We start families and we start having a totally different emotional connection to the world. That is through our children. On hindsight it is hard to realize just how fast they grew up. First teeth, first steps, first words, diaper trained, off to school, and so forth. And then repeat the process for each child. Four times for us. I do recall my mother celebrating when my younger brother was finally out of diapers. It struck me a funny that she would be so excited about that fact. Not until my own kids were in diapers did I realize that she had 6 or 7 years of cleaning out diapers. (No disposables in those days). Likewise, one of the happiest I had ever seen my dad was the day he came in the house from work in the summer of 1969 saying the house was paid for. His highest payment was $96 a month. But, it's all relative.

The good things like a last day of school, have an emotion attached to them and the event can be reflected upon.

However, there will be a time when you reflect on your life and your kids growing up that you realize may of the things that were part of your daily routine have not happened for a while. In fact, will never happen again.

Tucking a kid into bed, reading a good night story, singing a good night song ("The sun will come up tomorrow"), a night time prayer. What happened to those events? They just stopped. Your child could read themselves, could tuck themselves in, and could brush their own teeth. And besides, you had a younger child now to give your attention.

At one point we had a game of flying our kids up to bed. This may have started out as Superman, but eventually it became a helicopter. I would cup my hands in front of me and the tiny bottom would then sit in my cupped hands. The child would then hold each of my thumbs as pilot controls and they could fly their way upstairs to bed while I tried to simulate the chopper sounds. I probably did this with my younger three kids. However, with each kid there was a last flight. It was without ceremony and without knowing at the time. It may not have been until years later with grandkids that I even recalled doing this. So now my own kids put their kids to bed this way. And maybe sing "Tomorrow". (Or something from "Frozen").

There are many "last times" that involve our children. Flying to bed just happens to be my favorite. How about the last time you meet a child off the school bus, or make a peanut butter sandwich, or drive them to a good friends house, or stay up all night waiting for a fever to break, or holding their hand as you cross the street, or having lunch with them at school, or helping them with their multiplication tables with flash cards, or reading a story, or............

Everyone can come up with their own list of "last times". More recently I retired. My last day ever of work was memorable. I don't recall my last agent phone call or my last official email, but I do recall the party and "celebration" of my departure. However, I had to reflect on many last days at work over the years as I moved on to other jobs, relocations, and in a couple of instances face the realization that the choice was not mine. So, some of my last days were planed and a couple not.

The last time I saw each of my parents I knew it would be the last time. My dad had failing health for years and each time I left from a visit I would see him sitting in his chair and giving me a wave and a smile as I left the house. I often felt that would be my last image of my dad. However, I did see him in a care facility bed just before Christmas of 2004. I had to get back to Indiana for my job and Christmas with my family. Dad died on January 5.

It was similar with my mom. However, the last time I saw her she was now sitting in my dad's chair and dying of cancer. I had spent a week with her with daughter Kristin. It was a week I am glad I spent. She had good moments and some coughing spells that were not so good. But I left knowing it was the last time I would see her and knew she was in the good hands of hospice and my brother and sister. She died less than week later in the bedroom I had as a young child.

A few months later we were selling the house. We had an estate sale and most of the furniture was sold as well as a lot of the small stuff. I recall standing in the empty living room knowing it was the last time I would be there. This was the summer of 2005 after my folks had lived there for 56 years. I was nine months old in 1949 when we moved in.

Those are emotional last times that I knew were coming and was prepared for. My sister was more emotional about the house than I was. I knew we had our memories and that was all I needed. There was not going to be any new memories of that house that would replace those of my youth.

Now I am a grandfather. We live apart from our kids so only see the grandkids every few months. That is not recent enough for us to become part of their daily routine. I doubt we will experience the "last time experiences" that we had with our own kids. Instead our kids will experience their own memories and someday will reflect on their own "last times".

THE PEOPLE YOU TOUCH

We may not realize just how many different people we touch in a lifetime. A touch may be a handshake or people being squeezed together on an elevator. Some touches are intentional, and some are not. Then there are the emotional touches. We have not physically touched them but have met and have a shared experience. Some people we interact with and touch just by knowing.

In our lives we will touch upwards of tens of thousands of people. The remarkable thing is we recognize many or remember many of these people when we see them again. There are people from our youth that if we were to see today, we would recall memories and see that person from years ago in our mind.

The first people we really touch is our family. Parents, brothers and sisters, grandparents, and baby-loving aunts. They are the main people in our lives when we are young. It is interesting to put in perspective just what that really means to us. Let's consider grandparents. All four of my grandparents were born from 1880 to 1891. (None of my great-grandparents were still alive when I was born). I was born in 1948. My oldest grandfather was almost 70 when I was born. He held me, like any grandparent would do, and I probably looked at the strange old face and maybe wrapped my hand around his finger, as babies do. He was doing the same thing his grandfather did with him in the "old country"; a grandfather born in the early 1800's. In addition to touching people you are also placing yourself in time. My grandfather would live another 15 years. We called him "Pa". (Born in Sweden he had lots of grandkids before me.) All my cousins probably shared their connection to the past by touching him as I did.

My kids all had their picture taken with my grandmother. She was born in 1891 and lived to be 96. My youngest son only met her once when he was only a few weeks old.

After family the next big influence is your school. Kindergarten mixes you with 25 other five-year old's, most who you did not know before the first day of school. Yet years later you still know some of them. At my 40th class reunion there were 7 or 8 from my kindergarten class there for a group picture! By the time you get to high school you can recognize all your classmates. My friend Danny Lilleness, and I sat next to each other at our graduation. There were only two, in a class of 500, who we did not know before their name was called. We also knew many of the kids from the classes ahead of us or behind. I have no idea how many of my classmates actually knew who I was, but I am guessing most did. While you don't know everyone in school you immediately recognize a stranger when they show up in the group. New kid in school!

College adds to the number of people you know. Some of your best life friends may have come from college, but people come and go so fast that it is hard to really know the total number of people you touched in college. If you live in dorms you saw different students come and go each year. Many who started with you don't finish. Conversely, many of us met our futures spouses in college. The importance of the relationships was major at that point in time. My roommates were in, or at, my wedding.

When you enter the workforce you have a chance in a career to touch a huge number of people. The first office I worked had about 120 people. I knew all their names and remember lots still today. Then you move on and start all over again. I had a staff of 75 people who reported to me before I was 30. I knew every person and had a say in how their career advanced as other people did with mine.

Depending on your job or career you may have the opportunity to meet hundreds or even thousands more. I worked for companies with thousands of employees. Getting your name or picture in the company magazine could make you known to many of those folks, even without personally meeting them. I probably met 5000 different people in my 40-year insurance career.

In later years I gave many presentations to peers in the insurance industry. I often spoke to several hundred people for an hour on some boring topic. I have no idea how many of those people would

remember me in five years, but some will. Especially, when I attended the same conferences periodically.

Imagine the teacher who has 150 kids in their classes every semester. 300 a year. Times that by as many years as they teach. While they will not remember them all they will remember many and may end up teaching kids of students they had 25 years earlier.

Having a family opens you up to getting to know all your children's friends. School and sports will introduce you not only to your kid's friends or fellow competitors, but also their parents. My wife was administrator for our local youth sports club. There were upwards of 5000 families as members. A large percentage knew her as was witnessed when we would be out to dinner and a stranger would come up and complain about the coach their child just was assigned in soccer, etc. I was Commissioner of Baseball. Every spring there were 1200 kids who participated in ages 5-18. With my own three boys spread out over eight years I had a chance to know hundreds of young athletes and their families. Some are still very good friends of ours.

Different occupations present different situations. If I had lived my whole life in a small town with a small employer, the numbers would look a lot different.

It would be a wild guess to know the total number of people I touched in over 60+ years.

Now let's move on a bit. Imagine you are a 70-year-old grandfather holding your grandchild as your grandfather held you. He looks up into your eyes with a look of wonder. He wraps his hand around your finger and gives you a squeeze and maybe if you are lucky you will get a smile. When that baby holds his own grandchild in the later years of the 21st century more than 200 years will have passed from the birth of the grandfather who held you when you were a baby. One person "you" spans five or more generations and touched someone alive in the 1800s' as well as someone who may live to see 2100! My own kids have a better chance of doing this than me. They knew a great grandparent who was born in 1891. When they become grandparents or even great grandparents, they will touch someone who will live well into the 22nd century. A single person touching four centuries of life.

While we sometimes focus on the people who go through life with us (classmates, fellow employees), it takes the family relationship to span centuries. All with just a touch.

The purpose of all this is to let every reader reflect on the impact someone has in their lifetime. It is not insignificant. Keep in mind if there was no Pa then I would not have been. Every person has a chance to touch thousands of people in their lives. Some in a quick, forgettable handshake; others connecting the generations to us, both past and future.

I am just one of millions of baby boomers. We all could tell a similar story. Because we were born basically in the middle of a century it makes the numbers sound more impressive when reaching from 1880 to 2101. You could say that one person could actually touch people alive in four different centuries and not even live to be 100. It just takes that one grandchild that you now hold to live to 2101. Not a stretch with today's medicine.

You should not take lightly of the significance of the people you touch.

PART 2

LIDSTROM FAMILY HISTORY

Ron and Ole Lidstrom around 1927

LIDSTROM
FAMILY HISTORY

The following narrative and pictures are a summary of the Lidstrom family from the perspective of the grandchildren (including me), of Oscar and Hilma (Flink) Lidstrom. To be called "Pa" and "Ma" in this narrative. This was prepared for my sister, brother and first cousins.

There is much more family information available, so this is limited to our grandparents, their parents, their siblings, and our father. Ma and Pa were each from families of 8 kids that lived to adulthood. Pictures exist of almost all their siblings at the time of this writing. I will continue to add any other pictures to our collection if they come available.

Many of us met some of our grandparent's siblings. However, some of those meetings were when we were quite young so how these folks were actually related may not have been obvious at the time. Nor, as young children, did we probably care. The age range of all the cousins is extensive. Eleanor (my dad's oldest sister), already had cousins 15 years older than her when she was born in 1910. Our parents were part of a family spanning over 17 years of children from Eleanore to Patricia. Aunt Pat was born in 1927. Pa's siblings ranged in birth from 1871 to 1889. Ma's siblings ranged in birth from 1883 to 1906! As a result, our parent's cousins spanned many years.

OSCAR LIDSTROM'S PARENTS, BROTHERS AND SISTERS

Pa's parents, John and Elizabeth (Betty) were both born in Sweden and immigrated to northern Minnesota in the late 1880's. John was born in 1848, Betty in 1851. They were married in 1871, the same year their oldest daughter Minnie was born. Family stories say that John brought the family over in several groups and his wife Betty waited back in Sweden until the youngest children were old enough to travel on the ocean voyage. It appears the last group came over in 1892. That included Pa, his brother John, and the young twins, Vern and Ellen. They were born in 1889 so would only have been three years old for that trip. The Lidstrom homestead was a few miles south of Aitken, Minnesota. I am not even sure as to how many acres they had, but the existing farm is probably around 160 acres. They were on a hill. To the north were hay fields. Below, to the south, was a lake and near the lake the Lutheran Church. John Lidstrom is not listed as one of the original members of the church, but it is believed he helped build later additions, like the steeple. There is a cemetery at the church were John, Betty, and four of Pa's siblings are buried.

On the homestead a school was built. That was probably in the 1890's as I have seen a picture of Vern and Ellen as young students there. I do not have that picture in my collection. The School was called the "Lidstrom School". So, when my dad talked about the miles he had to walk to school he was telling tales. The school had not been used for many years and was destroyed by arson around 2010.

There are a couple of pictures of the farm. There was a brochure made to promote Aitken County, Minnesota and the family farm was featured on the cover. Steve Jacobs (who married Pa's sister Ellen) was riding a horse-drawn hay rake, or some sort of equipment. You can see the house and school in the background on the hill. The other picture (included), is from the farm yard itself. It is impossible to recognize who the people are. We can only speculate that they included John and Betty.

Lidstrom Family Homestead near Aitkin Minnesota, Around 1900

John and Elizabeth (Betty) Lidstrom. My Great Grandparents

So, what did they farm? Probably just enough to feed the family and livestock. There were lots of woods in the area that provided a nice supply of firewood. They did not have indoor plumbing nor electricity while they lived there. The house was heated by the wood stove in the kitchen. The kids who slept upstairs would take warmed bricks to bed with them to help stay warm in the winter. There would be icicles hanging from the ceiling on cold mornings. The farm was not a source of major income. Instead Pa and his brothers worked in the nearby iron ore mines. Some are still operational in the area and are very large open pit mines. I don't know how they got to their work, or if they boarded there. That would be interesting history to find out as the distance was probably 15 to 20 miles to the mines.

I am guessing that Anton took over the homestead when John died in 1907. Pa would have been 27 years old at the time and close to being married. Eventually Anton bought a neighboring farm, so our dad lived and grew up on the homestead until they moved to Seattle. Great grandma Betty lived there until she died in 1926. My dad remembered her. All of Pa's oldest siblings (Except Anton) were girls and probably moved away when they were married. Anton never married and lived on his farm until he died in 1950. The Wilber Nelson family now owns both tracks of land and farm turkeys. Wilber was probably Ole's age and a friend of my dad.

Let's see Pa's family. We have seen pictures of John Lidstrom and of Betty. None that I have show them together. Likewise, there are no group pictures of Pa and his siblings as youngsters. If Eleanore had any pictures of that nature they would have burned in their farm fire in 1954. Also, there was quite an age difference as already stated. The oldest sister, Minnie, would have been 18 when Vern and Ellen were born. She was probably married and out of the house when the younger kids finally immigrated in 1892.

1. The oldest of Pa's sisters was Minnie (Wilhelmina). She was born in Sweden in 1871. She is buried in the church cemetery at Aitkin. Minnie died in 1956. I only have one very old picture of her. She out-lived 2 husbands and then after her sister Mary died in 1918, she married Gus West. Mary had been married to Gus. Minnie would have raised her own children plus those of Mary after she passed.

2. Anton was the oldest son, born in 1873. He farmed near the family farm and died in 1950 having never married. There is a very good portrait of Anton that was probably taken in his 20's. My dad tells how Uncle Anton liked to drink. He would take the horse into town and the horse would bring him home.

3. Emma was born in 1875. I do not have a picture of Emma, but I think there probably is one that I will add to the collection in the future. She married Charles Nyman and is also in the Aitken cemetery. She died in 1942.

Around 2008 I met one of her daughters, Evelyn. She was 93 and living on her own in an apartment in Ironton, MN, just next to Crosby. She was 5 years younger than Eleanore, but recalls being close to her and staying on the Lidstrom farm in the summers as a girl. She recalled my dad as a kid and knew his cheek scar was a result of an accident involving the wood burning stove in the kitchen. Evelyn has since passed away.

4. Mary was born in 1877 and married Gus West. There is a very nice portrait of Gus, Mary and all their kids. My Dad's cousin Ellen West lived in Portland and I recall visiting her about once a year as a kid when we were in town. I also recall meeting her sister Hazel. It appears Mary died in the 1918 influenza epidemic along with her daughter Gertrude. It was after her death that Gus married Minnie who must have helped raise the younger children. Mary, Minnie and Gus are all together in the cemetery.

5. Oscar "Pa" was born in 1880 and moved to Minnesota in 1892. He was 12 years old. I know nothing of his schooling. He and Ma married in 1907. As a young man he also worked the mines. There is 1905 Wisconsin census where he can be found with his brothers John and Anton. They were all listed as minors. I am guessing they went over to Wisconsin to find work and it while there that he met Ma. Her dad and other family members also worked the mines. Pa and Ma moved to Seattle in 1940 after giving up the farm. Pa died in early 1964 and is buried in Seattle.

6. John was born in 1882 and died in 1941, still in Minnesota. He also married a Hilma. They had six kids and many of us knew

Sheldon, Warren, and Audrey. Most of those families moved to Washington State.

There is a good group picture of the six of the John and Hilma Lidstrom kids. Perhaps from their dad's funeral.

7-8. Vern and Ellen were born in in Sweden in 1889 and were twins. Vern married Orpha and they moved to Seattle prior to the rest of the family. Orpha's family was already there. I knew her two brothers, Bud and Lester Pickett. They were Seattle cops. Vern and Orpha lived on Beacon Hill and I would see them a couple of times a year when my dad would visit. Their son Bob was a close friend of my dad before the war. There are pictures from Vern's 50th wedding anniversary with my dad and his Cousin Bob. Vern died in 1974 and is buried in Seattle.

Ellen married Steve Jacobs and stayed in Minnesota. Their son Melvin took over his dad's farm and I recall visiting them in 1961. One of Melvin's daughter's is Ellen Bovee lived on their farm until she passed away in 2019. Pa's sister Ellen died in 1954. Her husband Steve lived well into his 80's.

HILMA FLINK LIDSTROM'S PARENTS AND BROTHERS AND SISTERS

Ma and her siblings were all born in the Ironwood, Michigan area. Her father, Esaias Flink and mother, Charlotta Elionora Norin were born in Sweden.

Esaias was nick named Pee Pa. He was born in Sweden in 1860 and immigrated to the US about 1881 and worked in the Iron Ore Mines around Ironwood, Michigan. He then homesteaded the area on Lake Superior (Little Girls Point) about 15 miles north of Ironwood, in about 1888 and would live there for the next 52 years. Pee Pa made the first trail from Ironwood to the lake and named all the streams. Including "Wet Ass Creek", one that he apparently fell in. This area is just a few miles from the Wisconsin state line. Charlotte (we will call her that however, we see her with other iterations of her name), was born in Sweden in 1864 and probably also came to America around 1880 or 1881.

They married in July of 1882 in Florence Wisconsin. If correct Charlotte was only 18.

There are pictures of Pee Pa and Charlotte, but like John and Betty Lidstrom, none together. The area they homesteaded is heavily wooded and settling there would involve clearing large sections of forest to grow hay and the like. Lumber, mining, and fishing were sources of family income during this time. They did not earn an income from farming. Wood would be cut for fuel and some eventually it made its way to the huge paper mills on Lake Michigan. A couple of Ma's brothers fished on Lake Superior. They would sell their fish for restaurants in Chicago, etc. It is amazing with roads and transportation the way it was 100 years ago how they could make a living and have a market for their catch. So mining, lumber and fishing were the family sources of income. Like the Lidstrom's, in Minnesota, you could say they lived on farms, but did not make much from farming. As homesteaders they got the land for free as long as they live there and made some improvements eventually becoming true owners.

Pee Pa looked larger than life in his pictures and based on family stories. As stated, he cleared the first road from Ironwood to Little Girls Point and named most of the landmarks and creeks. It could not have been an easy life, yet they had eight kids. Almost all stayed in the area and lived on land adjoining the original homestead. Ma was the only one to move totally away. Most are buried in the Ironwood Cemetery.

Charlotte died in 1920 in Ironwood. She was 56 years old and had given birth to eight children who lived to adulthood and at least one who died as an infant. Pee Pa out lived her by 20 years. He died in 1940 after a long illness. They are both buried at the Ironwood cemetery.

Flink homestead, Ironwood, Michigan

Esaias Flink, "Pee Pa"   Charlotta Elionore Norin Flink,
My Great Grandmother

I do not know where kids went to school. The youngest cousin of my Dad (Lucy) was born in 1945 and took a bus to school into town. There was an old school at the end of their lane that may have been the school at the time Ma went to school.

There is an extensive amount of research that has been done regarding all the members of the family. However, it is not my intention to go into that much detail here.

1. The first of Ma's sisters was Anna, born in 1883. Her mother, Charlotte, would have been 19. The place of birth was Stambaugh, Michigan. The maps show that is a township near Ironwood. That might be closer to where the mines were as they had not homesteaded yet. Anna Married Charles Parker in 1902 and died in Ashland, Wisconsin in 1959. I don't think I saw her grave marker when visiting the Ironwood Cemetery in June of 2016.

2. Oscar was born in 1885. Oscar married Anna West in 1912 and died at Little Girls Point in 1969. I don't recall if we saw Oscar when we visited the area in 1961. He is buried in the Ironwood Cemetery. His house is still standing on the road along the lake.

Flink Kids about 1898.
Back Row Standing: Anna, Oscar
Middle: Esther, Bud, Hilma (in chair), Ted,
Front: Lillian

3. Ma (Hilma) was the third born, just about the time they moved to Little Girls Point. She was born in July of 1889. She married Pa in 1907 and would have been 18 years old. Pa was 27. They then settled in Minnesota and in 1940 moved to Seattle. She died in a Seattle hospital from complications from diabetes in 1954. When Pa was courting Ma, he would leave his calling card. I have a copy of one of these cards. Very formal. I don't know how they would "date" when she lived 15 miles north of town, through the woods.

4-5. After Ma twins were born in 1891. Esther and Lillian. They lived their entire lives in that area. Lillian married William Kellett. Of their children, Norman Kellett was popular with my dad and we visited them in 1961. Their house, right on Lake Superior, is still in the family. The youngest of their kids, Jean, is still alive and over 90 years old and lives in Arizona. Lillian did have a second marriage to Axel Moberg in 1941. She died in 1946. She lived in town when she died and is buried in the Ironwood cemetery.

Her twin Esther married Enoch Dixon in 1912 and she died in August 1961. At her death she lived in a newer house on the original homestead. We visited there in July 1961 and I believe Esther is who we met. The forest is taking over that property. The original homestead house is gone (the house my dad was born in). The wood barn is there, but very hard to get to. Likewise, the newer house can only be reached either in the winter when the ground is frozen or fall when the ground dries up. You cannot see the house through the trees on the lot and it is too wet to wade through the woods and ticks.

6. Ted was born in 1894 and was a veteran of WWI. He died in 1979. We stayed with them in 1961 in their house in Hurley, WI. His first wife had died, and he had remarried when we saw him in 1961. He is buried in the Ironwood Cemetery.

7. Leonard "Bud" was next in 1896. He married Ruth Johnson in 1924. He may have also had a second wife, Irene. We visited him at his strawberry farm a couple of miles down the road from the homestead along the lake. The land still has a working berry farm, but not in the family. Bud is also buried in the Ironwood cemetery. I have a business card for his berry patch that he gave me in 1961.

8. Then 10 years later Carl Henry was born. That was 1906. He is not in the family picture of the other seven children. He also lived just south of the homestead and married Agnes Long in 1933. We also visited them in 1961. Two of his kids are still alive. Carl Jr. and Lucile (Lucy). Lucy has been my source for many of the pictures and the family tree information. She and her husband still spend a couple of weeks a year on her family's farm. It also is very overgrown. It has electricity, but no indoor toilet. Likewise, the stove is the only heat source. They really rough it when they visit. But it does keep them connected to that area. Lucy and Mike actually live in Omaha, NE. Carl and Agnes are also buried in the Ironwood cemetery.

There was one other child, a boy, born at some point between 1896 and 1906. I am not sure if there are even any birth or death records. It is just family knowledge.

LIDSTROM CHILDREN

So, Ma and Pa had six children. Ma and Pa were married in August of 1907, in Ironwood, Michigan. That would have been Ma's home. Recall that Pa had been working the mines there in 1905. At some point they did move back to the homestead in Aitken as John Lidstrom also died in 1907. There was an adopted baby Doris that appears on the 1910 census and in some early pictures. Her name is shown as Lidstrom, but it is doubtful that Ma and Pa were her parents. She is gone by 1920. There is no Doris that shows up as an adult in the family records.

1. Eleanore (Auntie Lala), was born in Cuyuna, Minnesota in July of 1910. Cuyuna is near Crosby, where the mines were. Eleanore married Art Degnan in June of 1931. She was 21 when she married. I don't know where they lived after they got married but my dad had several stories of life on the farm that included Art. Their daughter Patty was born in 1932 and another girl, Shirley Jean was born in 1934. She died as an infant and is buried in the Aitken church cemetery. They had a dairy farm and moved to Washington State at the end of the war. Art worked in the Bremerton Navy Yard until he retired. After Patty they had four boys, the youngest born in 1951. Lala died in 1993.

2. Melvina (Mel or Mina) was born in 1915 in Ironton, which is also right next to Crosby. I am guessing the hospital was there. If they were born on the farm, I don't know what the birth certificate would show. At some point I will track down actual birth records. She married Charles Baker in the late 30's. They also made it out to Seattle about the same time as the rest of

the family. Pete is Mina's son. His story was a family secret for years. We have since made the shift from uncle to cousin. He was explained as an adopted son of Ma and Pa when we were younger. Mickey, Penny, and Butch were all Baker's. Recent information shows Mina also gave a baby up for adoption in 1948. No father is listed on the birth record. She was no longer with Chuck Baker at that time. Mina married Ed Hansen in the 50's and lived in Portland until she died in 1990.

3. Ole (Lawrence) was born in 1919 in Crosby. There are two stories that define his early years. He was kicked in the head by a horse as a child and was in a coma for quite some time. He had to learn to walk and talk all over again once he became conscious. He was probably just a couple of years old when that happened. He also had Rheumatic Fever as a child which affected his heart and probably was the cause of his early death in 1945. Today we know that Rheumatic Fever is an advanced stage of the strep virus. Simple antibiotics can check it. I doubt any of these kids saw a doctor very often.

I only know of two pictures that include Ole. One is as a boy taken with my dad Ronnie. The other is with older sister Mina, Chuck Baker, Mickey and Penny. He lived in Seattle when he died so probably came out with the rest of the family. He was engaged when he died and I believe the ring was returned as it was destroyed in the Degnan farm house fire. Due to his bad heart he was not able to do heavy work. When cutting firewood on the farm he would hold down one end of the log while dad did the sawing. I have not seen his obituary.

4. Ronnie was born in his mother's family old homestead home in Ironwood, Michigan. That was September 1921. That house was the original homestead house of the Flink's. His mother would have lived there while growing up. She must have been back for a visit when the baby was born. That house was just torn down in the last few years. Like most of the kids he never finished school. He quit school at 16 as he needed to work to help the family. He moved with the family to Seattle in 1940. He recalls that they did enjoy some of the sights, such as Mt. Rushmore, along the way. He joined the Marine Corps in 1942

and once shipped overseas he did not return home until he was released from the hospital in Astoria in 1946. He met my mom while working as a pen repairman for a small stationary store in downtown Seattle. His boss was Blake Rolston, also a vet., and Blake was married to my mom's sister. Mom had moved to Seattle from Philadelphia in 1946 and met my dad at a New Year's party. The rest is history. They married in September 1947 and I was born in December 1948. Nancy and John were born in 1951 and 1953.

5. Norma was born February 28, 1925. Or was it 1924? Her grave marker says 1925, but other family records show 1924. She was also born in Crosby. She would have been about 15 or 16 when they moved to Seattle. Norma died in 2000 and I have no contact with her daughters Beverly and Patsy. I cannot confirm her actual birth year with them. She married Clayton Powers (Mike) and they both lived in the same area of Seattle near Columbia City until they died.

6. Patricia was born in 1927 and would have been 13 when they moved to Seattle. Her birth place is listed as Ironton, MN. Again, just next to Crosby. Pat also had a bad heart; however, it may have been something from birth. She could not have children as it was not believed her heart could take childbirth. She was found dead at the bus stop, on her way to work, in 1957, just 30 years old. Pat was married to Hal Wittmeyer, who remained close to the family until he died around 2010. I am guessing that Pat went to Franklin High School, in Seattle, and would have graduated in 1945. Pat and Hal were my God Parents.

Both Norma and Pat were married in 1948.

Lidstrom cousins are:

Patricia Degnan (Hovde)
Shirley Jean Degnan (died as an infant)
Lance Degnan
Bruce Degnan
Tom Degnan
Dennis Degnan

Keith "Pete" Lidstrom
Chuck "Mickey" Baker
Penny Baker
Richard "Butch" Baker
Robert Ginn (adopted name)

Bruce Lidstrom
Nancy Lidstrom
John Lidstrom

Beverly Powers
Patsy Powers

All are alive except Pat Hovde and Penny.

Summary

Mike Lewis (Cousin Lucy's Flink's husband) has done considerable work on the Flink side of the family and has records from Sweden going back to the 1600's. Sorry, no pictures going back that far. As stated, I have taken the work done by our cousin DiAnn Lidstrom (Sheldon's daughter), my sister Nancy, Mike Lewis, and Ellen Bovee to put all this together. Ellen has put together a wonderful scrapbook on the Lidstrom side of her family. Many of these pictures came from her scrapbook. Most information has been verified by actual birth, death, and marriage records. I can share any detail to anyone who wishes to go into this in more detail. For example, DiAnn Lidstrom Easterby has taken records down to all the second cousins and all our kids at the time of her research. It is not complete, but very interesting. Someday I may try to contact some distant cousins that I recall as kids. Time is running out on us.

Hope you enjoyed the trip back through our family history.

Bruce Lidstrom
July 2016

Ma and Pa and baby Doris around 1910

Oscar Lidstrom, "Pa"   Hilma Lidstrom, "Ma"

John Lidstrom, second from right.

PART 3

AMERICAN TOUR
AMTRAK TRAIN TRIP
BRUCE LIDSTROM
SEPTEMBER/OCTOBER 2015

When someone gets close to retirement one of the general questions a prospective retiree must answer is, "Do you have any travel plans?" Over the years I have seen retirees come back into the office with their photo books of Hawaii and similar trips. All very nice. Except I have already been to Hawaii. In fact, I have been to a lot of places. So, a special retirement trip did not seem anything special. Not only that but my wife Connie, is not retired. We have new grandkids that need visiting and she will not "waste" vacation time to take a trip that could repeat things we have already done.

We have been to all the states. We have seen London, Paris, and Rome. We have done cruises and been to two of the Hawaiian Islands. This is not saying we will not do another cruise or go back to Hawaii, but not for my retirement. However, I felt I would let people down by doing nothing.

Over the last few years we have talked about doing the Amtrak trip between Minnesota and Seattle. At least one direction and then fly the other. We would get a sleeper car and enjoy the sights of Glacier National Park in Montana. However, considering the grandkid references above and family weddings, among other things, it would not be easy to fit in. Not only that, Connie probably does not enjoy visiting Seattle as much as I do. I stay at a friend's house or my brothers. Connie would be more comfortable at a hotel, but that of course adds to the expense of the trip. So, we never set a date to do such a trip. The closest we have come to discussing such a possible trip was maybe something tied into my 50th high school class reunion. That would be in Seattle, however, not until 2017.

At some point I did go on-line to see information on Amtrak trips. Route maps showed that their trains covered a large percentage of the country. There are only a few states they do not travel to and they may have local spurs that accommodate those. I had heard a lot of stories of people traveling through Europe using a Euro Rail pass. Turns out Amtrak has something similar. They have passes for multiple travel legs that must be covered in a given time span. For example, 12 legs in 30 days. A "leg" ends at the end of a route or when you get off somewhere prior to the end of the route. When you re-board you start a new leg. It sounded interesting. So interesting in fact, that I started mentioning it as a possibility for when I retired.

I have had some travel by train. Before I had a car in college, I would sometimes take the train home from school on weekends. The trip was about 2 ½ hours and probably cost less than $3.00. It was always a nice trip and the train went along the shores of Puget Sound from Bellingham with nice water and mountain views coming into Seattle. I remember a train ride I took with my mom around 1958. We went to Snoqualmie Falls from Seattle and back, being pulled by an old steam locomotive. (With aid from a diesel locomotive in the rear). Of interest to a 9-year-old was the fact that when you flushed the toilet you were offered a view of the rail ties under the train.

We took the kids on Amtrak when living in Orange County, Ca. around 1982. We went up into Los Angeles where Union Station was walking distance to the Children's Museum. Also, in 2008 I rode a dinner train out of Lewiston, Montana. This was part of a small convention of mutual insurance companies I was attending. The train was robbed by bandits on horseback, so it was a fun trip. Another nice trip is the old train between Hill City and Keystone in the Black Hills of South Dakota.

When I worked in San Francisco I took the train to and from work. BART was easy and saved driving into the city. That was from 1976 to 1978. Likewise, when visiting New York, I would take the train into the city from New Jersey. Of my time in Europe my longest train ride was from London to Dover and back. Plus, the London Underground so I had some rail experience, but nothing like what I was planning.

My retirement date was April 30, 2015. I had turned 66 the prior December but did not want to retire in the winter. If I wanted to do this train trip, I figured I would plan it for the fall after peak tourist season, but still good weather and daylight. Eventually, many of my co-workers and all my family knew of my intentions. Now, I had committed myself and was going to have to do something. The trip would circle the entire country by train. New England, to Florida to California, to Seattle and home to Minnesota.

In May 2013 I had visited my brother and his family in Seattle. Nephew Nick was finishing his freshman year of high school at that time. Nick played football and I made the commitment of seeing him play a game before he graduated in 2016. So that become one focal point of the trip. There would be about two months of weekly football games that I could base my Seattle stay around. There were other visiting situations that I also wanted to plan for. Connie's sister Patty and her husband Jim would be moving from New England to Florida at some point in late summer. Also, Connie's sister Debbie had recently moved to Florida from Seattle. My sister in Austin was indicating they were moving to Colorado. A niece, Christina, was getting married in Virginia in October. So how could I plan travel to see everyone at the times they were available?

I now had to contact those I wanted to visit along the way. It was going to be a challenge to work the train travel around seeing people. Two of my kids live in Indianapolis so that seemed a logical stop. Yet, the train arrives there around midnight and both my kids work. What would I do during the day? How would I get around? How much of my total number of days would that eat up? Plus, we see our kids frequently. Going through Indianapolis was not the best way to continue to Boston. Also, if I wanted to visit my sister in Texas. The closest my train came to Austin would be San Antonio, about 2 hours south of Austin. Either they pick me up in the middle of the night or I wait until the next day to take a connection line. To allow time for a visit and then get back to San Antonio to continue my route west could eat up 5 days or so.

As it turned out my sister and her husband did move to Colorado Springs. The best way to get to Denver was an east bound train out of Sacramento. However, the same situations applied regarding the round trip and getting around. That option would use two legs and probably 5, or more, calendar days that would eat into the number of total allowable days I had to work with. At planning time it was unclear as to if they would even be available, having just arrived there. As it turned out they didn't even have their furniture delivered yet when I would have visited.

One of the rules of using the US Rail Pass is that all tickets must be issued prior to the commencement of travel. So now I had to contact everyone I intended to visit to see if they would be available when I came through their area. Connie's brother Bob (north of Boston), was not available until the second weekend in September. Deciding on going clockwise or counter-clockwise around the country had to be looked at. It appeared that in going either direction I was not going to make the October 10 wedding in Virginia. The closest I would come would have me going through Charlottesville about three weeks before the wedding. I doubted they would change their wedding date. My friend Jeff, in Florida, had just started driving a cattle truck from

Florida to Texas. He could be out several days each week. So how do I gamble and plan time with him? Connie's sister Patty and her husband Jim would be staying at Debbie's apartment while they looked for a house in south Florida. Would she also have room for me?

Then I learned that Amtrak no longer goes directly from Orlando to New Orleans. To get to New Orleans I would have to backtrack, perhaps all the way to Washington DC., from Florida. My sister would definitely not be in Texas, so no stops there. My cousin Mickey would be in Oakland when I came through, but friends Karen and Galen would not be home in Sacramento. They would be on a 17-day Panama Canal Cruise. Cousin Butch was available in Portland.

Now for Seattle. I wanted to see a number of people. In addition to Nick's game, I wanted to see my college roommate Byron. We talked and decided to meet up at a Mariners game, which we had done several times in the past. I have a cousin Ronnie who I have not seen in about 40 years. He was just a kid when we moved away in 1976. It would work out best to try to meet up with him around his work schedule. His sister Laura would be in Hawaii. (She had offered me her lake cabin outside of Bremerton, but now that would not work). My high school friend Danny is where I usually stay, but his daughter was back from Norway and there was not room at his place. Then there was my nephew Jimmy Cotton and his five-year-old daughter Elsie, whom I had not met yet. And finally, our first next door neighbors (from 1975) Brad and Sue who had also just recently retired. It looked like I could meet up with all of them. So how long to stay in Seattle to see everyone?

While all this planning was going on, I got a "friend request" on Facebook from Byron's old college girlfriend Sue. Sue had dropped out of sight sometime in the 80's. Now she was retired and reaching out to contact old friends. Sue had eventually married Mike, whom I went to high school with. We had been to their wedding and did things with them until we moved away in 1976. We probably only saw her a few times after that. It was very nice to hear from Sue and we decided to take a day and go back and visit our college campus in Bellingham. Western Washington University. Then Sue asked if she could come to the ballgame and see her old boyfriend Byron. (You'll hear later how it all worked out.) My time in Seattle became fairly busy.

I probably spent parts of several days on the Amtrak website looking at departure and arrival times of each route I wanted to travel. It was an objective to minimize any hotel stays. However, I needed to allow time to make connections knowing trains often ran late. Friends and family had to be available to meet me when I got into a city.

Now how to book? I knew I had to purchase the rail pass. Then a call to Amtrak would be needed to acquire a reservation for each leg. I decided to use a local travel agent to help with that part of the plan. Through all my planning I was looking at a 15 leg/ 45-day pass. However, some things helped to reduce that. A couple people would not be available to visit thus not requiring a stop. Suddenly it looked like I could do the entire trip using 13 legs and in 30 days. I would pay for the 13th leg separately. Just find the shortest/cheapest leg and that would be covered independent of the Rail Pass.

The cost of a 30-day pass was $698. About $200 less than the 45-day pass. The total trip would be just over 10,000 miles. There would be nine nights on a train. Two of the legs covered spans of two days and two nights. (New Orleans to LA and Seattle to Minn.). I would look into buying a sleeper car berth for each of those legs. The sleeper for the southern route was about $350 extra and the northern route was $210. So, the entire trip would come to about $1300. One thing that also made a sleeper attractive was that meals were included. I would regret not having a couple of more sleeper car nights once travel began. More on that later.

The travel agent spent an hour on the phone with Amtrak in setting the trip up. From that I realized I had misread routes and did not have to go through New York City to get to Boston. (A good thing). Also, I made the final decision to get a sleeper for the New Orleans to Los Angeles leg. (A good choice). Finally, I was booked. Now I needed actual tickets in hand. The travel agent could not issue tickets. The closest Amtrak station (where I was starting my trip from) was St. Cloud, MN. However, St. Cloud was not a ticket issuing station. It was a limited service station. I had to make a special trip to St. Paul to get tickets issued for each leg of my trip. Now what was I going to do with $1300 of negotiable tickets? We'd figure something out. The tickets were issued on August 19. My travel would start the Wednesday after Labor Day on September 9.

The route looked like this

> St. Cloud, MN to Chicago. Five-hour layover in Chicago
> Chicago to Albany NY. Crossed over to the Boston train in Albany

Albany to Boston. Meet my brother-in-law Bob and stay weekend in Concord, NH.

Boston to New York. About 3-hour layover in New York

New York to West Palm Beach, FL. Stay with sister-in-law Debbie

West Palm Beach to Orlando, Fl. Stay with friend Jeff on sailboat near Coco Beach

Orlando to Washington DC. Sightsee in DC. Must backtrack to get to New Orleans

Washington DC to New Orleans. Stay in hotel two nights waiting for LA train.

New Orleans to Los Angeles. 5-hour layover in LA

LA to Oakland. Planned to visit my cousin Mickey in Oakland

Oakland to Portland, OR. Planned to visit my cousin Butch (Mickey's brother)

Portland to Seattle. Spend 6 days visiting friends and family

Seattle to St. Cloud, MN. Home

That was a total of 13 legs. The Rail Pass covered 12 so I bought a separate ticket for the Portland to Seattle trip for about $25.

One change had to be made once my travel started. Cousin Mickey's wife told me via Facebook that Mickey would not be in Oakland when I came through. Instead, he would be at his house on the Oregon coast. I got hold of him and his brother in Portland and was able to change my plans while I was still traveling in the east. I would skip the Oakland stop and go straight from LA to Portland. Butch would pick me up and we would drive to Depoe Bay on the coast and stay with Mickey. This worked out very well and was a very enjoyable part of the trip. The change was easy to make for Amtrak and it did not really affect anything else.

After getting my tickets I had some time to prepare for the trip. Since the travel was now cut down to 30 days I was going to be back in Minnesota on Thursday, October 8. If we planned things right, we would be able to get to the wedding in Charlottesville, VA on the 10th. That would be a road trip and entailed about 20 hours of driving each way. Doable.

Since the train comes through St. Cloud at 5:15 in the morning and St. Cloud is over 2 hours from Marshall we would need a hotel room the night before I left and the night before I got back. Connie would take me to St. Cloud, spend the night, drop me off early in the morning, and be back in Marshall in time to get to work. Likewise, when I returned, she would pick me up and we would start our trip to Virginia right from St. Cloud.

The train from New Orleans to Los Angeles only runs three days a week. Most other routes run daily. Just the bad luck of timing would mean I would have to stay there two nights. I made those hotel reservations near the French Quarter.

I wanted to travel light. One bag for my clothes and a backpack. I took only casual clothes. Hopefully I would get to do laundry at several points along the way, so I didn't take more than a weeks' worth of clothes. While I ended up only checking my bag on a couple of legs, I had all my personal stuff in a backpack. That included cameras, a "tablet" for email, medicine, books, a Kindle, puzzle books, and travel information. Connie made a "money belt" to wear under my jeans. That was were extra cash and all those tickets could be kept.

Right before I left I contacted everyone again to advise that I really was going to come and visit them and made sure I had their email address and phone numbers with me. I don't have a smart phone. But I was able to text folks along the way and was in dialog with some folks through much of the trip. I borrowed Connie's tablet. I had to set up my email, learned how to use the camera feature and how to post pictures on Facebook, and a few other things.

All my bills were paid about a month in advance. Most are automatic, but a couple needed individual checks, so I made arrangement for those to be paid. Likewise, using the tablet I could check my bank balance along my route. The Amtrak website made several references to Wi-Fi on the trains. Otherwise, I assumed the depots had Wi-Fi as well as places I stayed. It did not always work out the way I hoped, but I was able to make an internet connection most days.

So now it was just waiting the last few days to start my trip. I have traveled a lot in my life and for the most part it is no big deal for me. However, I found myself getting very apprehensive about this trip. Uncharacteristically so. I worried about trains running late and missing a connection (only three places where that could happen). I worried that for some reason there would be problems with my tickets. That was exasperated by a phone call recording I received saying if I did not pay for my tickets then all my reservations would be cancelled.

I had paid and when I called back I was reassured of that, but I got that recorded message two more times. I worried that I would lose my tickets, or they would be stolen. I worried about everyone being available to meet me when they said they would. For example, would Jeff be off driving truck and just not be there at all. I wondered how spending 9 nights on a train would affect my rest. And so forth. Even once travel started, I tended to focus more on the next connection than on sitting back and enjoying the trip. At least for a while.

There was one moment of humor associated with my anxiety. On August 17, Jeff called from the Orlando train station letting me know he was waiting for me just across the street from the depot. Only problem was I was not scheduled to arrive in Orlando until SEPTEMBER 17. Jeff was a full month early. We laughed and he was there again a month later.

On the late afternoon of September 8, Connie and I drove to St. Cloud MN. It was a little over a two-hour drive. It was still light when we got into town, so we first found the train station. It was on the east side of the Mississippi River. Our hotel was a Best Western on the west bank of the river. I found the best route from the hotel to the station and we knew it would only take a couple of minutes early the next morning. The train was scheduled to depart at 5:15am. I had been watching this train daily on-line and knew that it was rarely on time. However, we had to plan as if it would be. Connie really didn't need to wait for me to leave, but she would anyway. She still made it to work in plenty of time.

At the hotel it took a while to get an internet connection on my tablet, but by the time we went to bed we saw the train was running about an hour behind. That was normal. It just so happened that the premier showing of Stephen Colbert's new Late-Night Show was on that night. We had to watch that, even though I was recording it at home. Lights out around 11:30. I did not sleep that well as I didn't want to oversleep. I would get breakfast on the train and Connie would grab a fast food on her way home.

Trip Begins. Leg 1
September 9, 2015
8 Empire Builder
St. Cloud, MN to Chicago   486 Miles   10:41 hours
States: Minnesota, Wisconsin, Illinois

We got up at 4:15 and were at the station a little after 5:00. The Amtrak website was showing the train would arrive/leave closer to 6:00. In this case it is better to be an hour early than a minute late. There were only two other passengers waiting for the train outside in the dark. Plus, some Amtrak crew members. One of the other passengers was only going to the next stop at St. Paul. He was traveling with nothing. The other was a student going back to his school in Wisconsin. For the first of many times I described my trip. I would repeat the story countless times. However, everyone was always interested and had a lot of questions. Why was I doing this? How much did it cost? Was I going alone? Some joked about joining me.

At 6:00am (only 45 minutes late) the Empire Builder came into view. I said goodbye to my wife. The 30 days I would be away would probably be the longest away time of our 42-year marriage. The train had all double decker cars and we were directed to the upper level. Almost all passengers were asleep, and the car was very dark with just very dim ceiling lights on low. From the best I could see it looked like most passengers had two seats together and could spread out. I didn't want to have to impose and disturb someone by waking them to take their extra seat. However, at the front of the car I found a spot with two seats. There was plenty of room for my bags up above and I was on my first train. Out the window I saw my wife waiting for me to leave sitting in her car, but she could not see me in the darkness. Without a sound or a lurch the train smoothly pulled out of the station. All departures were that way. Since we were quite a way back from the engines we could not hear the rumble increase as it started to pull. Soon we were up to speed and I took a minute to get my bearings.

The conductor came by to take my ticket. Actually, they just scan it as most people have e-tickets. Based on the nature of my travel I had the old-fashioned airline type tickets; tab cards where the shorter end was separated as my receipt. However, the conductor still manually put a destination tag above the seat. Mine had "CHI" for Chicago. Looking around most said for "STP" for St. Paul.

The train ran parallel to old US highway 10 for a while. Several years ago, when I was still living in Indiana I spoke at a conference in Brainerd, MN. To return home I left the hotel about 4:30 in the morning to make the drive to the Minneapolis airport where I would fly back to Indianapolis. I recall passing the Amtrak that night. I could hear the whistle as it came to crossings and I was impressed by the length of the train and wondered where it had come from. That was in February of 2008. So here it was 7 ½ years later and I was on that train.

Seats are spacious. They are wider than an airline seat and there is also a lot of legroom. Seats reclined a lot and did not really bother the person behind. There was also a foot rest attached to the seat in front and a leg support that sprang up in the front of the seat like a recliner. If you had both seats to yourself you could sleep in some comfort. Getting two seats together was a big "if" on later trains. There was plenty of room overhead for bags, plus bags could be stowed below where we came on the train. Passengers could also check their bags and would not see them again until reaching their destination. St. Cloud did not have bag checking so I was carrying my bag and backpack on this train. A very nice feature were power outlets at each seat which made it easy to charge phones or plug in anything else.

The conductor told me the location of the dining car where breakfast was being served starting at 6:30. So at that time I had my first Amtrak meal. You are always seated with other passengers to make best use of limited space. On the more crowded trains reservations are needed, but usually not for the early breakfast eaters. I was seated with two older ladies (older than me) who were sisters. They were returning home to St. Paul where we were scheduled to arrive around 7:45am. They had been out to Glacier National Park in Montana and did that round trip frequently. They would spend several days in the park and then return. It sounded like a nice trip. The sisters shared a sleeper car and from their standpoint that was the only way they would ever travel while on a train. I told them my plans and they were concerned that I was spending 5 nights on trains without having a sleeper. Why would I do that? Over the trip I ran into a few other older people with the same sentiments and advise. They were not wrong.

The food was from a limited menu. It did get somewhat boring over the entire trip, but overall it was okay. Breakfast with eggs, potatoes, and a muffin was $9.00. Bacon or sausage was $3.00 more. With juice and coffee, you could spend about $15.00 just on breakfast. The sleeper car, with meals included in the ticket price, seemed practical already.

Back at my seat I watched half the passengers disembark at St. Paul. After that I moved to the left side of the car. I was hoping to have the sun behind me as I took pictures. However, even from the upper level I quickly found picture taking a challenge. This train had a dome car, but it was no higher than my own seat, so I stayed there to see the sights. I had a "guide book" which described all the features we would see along the way. It gave approximate distances from the last station. So, I usually knew where I was and could look out for interesting features before they came into view. Sometimes. The Empire Builder would continue along the Mississippi before crossing over into Wisconsin. From La Crosse we headed east to Milwaukee and then south along Lake Michigan to Chicago.

Once in Chicago I would get on another train heading east. We were scheduled to arrive in Chicago at 3:55 pm. The train did end up making up the time we were behind while going through Wisconsin and arrived in Chicago pretty much on time.

There are a couple of major themes on retelling this trip story. One is the actual train ride itself and the scenery. My expectation was for this feature to be the highlight. However, I soon realized that an interesting sidelight was the people I traveled with. Some I met and others I just observed. Many people were very interesting, and they did add flavor to the trip. I will introduce you to some of the characters I met along the way. A third factor was the things I did and people I visited on my stops. I had overnight stays in New England, Florida, New Orleans, Oregon, and Seattle. Each stay was interesting, and I got to see a lot of family and friends.

Meanwhile, after leaving St. Paul, the train traveled through some of nicest scenery I would see on the entire trip. I just didn't realize it at the time. The train ran along the Mississippi River. However, that stretch of the river had dams and fairly big reservoirs. The station at Red Wing was part of a city park which was very pretty. The station at Winona was worth a couple of pictures for the design of the depot. Between those two stations was 60 miles of river scenery and looking into the yards of very nice lake homes. These homes were not the typical houses you would see on most of the trip from the train. I could live in most of these places. Except a train ran through the yard. My guide book said Lake Pepin was home to a large eagle population. The book was right, but my camera was not quick enough in getting off a shot. As I looked up from my book, just off shore were at least 4 bald eagles circling. A beautiful sight.

The nice scenery continued through Wisconsin. However, when going through forest and wooded areas the view was just a lot of trees. I could not tell when a clearing might be coming that might be a nice shot. We went through La Crosse and Wisconsin Dells. Somewhere along this route I had lunch. It must have been uneventful as I don't recall who I ate with. I believe I did eat again in the dining car and probably had their burger. My next pictures were of downtown Milwaukee and then the ride south along Lake Michigan to Chicago. I had some good views of the Chicago skyline and the railyards. The commuter trains where getting ready for their afternoon runs so there was a lot of rail activity. I had taken trains into Chicago from the airports, but really had not been to their Union Station. As it turns out it was underneath a busy part of the business district along the Chicago River.

Chicago Layover

I wanted to post pictures of my trip on Facebook as I went along. I went outside and got some shots of the city. The river and bigger buildings. I had already checked my bag for the next leg. The layover was five hours and I didn't want to be toting a heavy bag around during that time. Unfortunately, the station common areas did not have Wi Fi. Nor did the Great Hall, the huge waiting area of the station. Meanwhile, I needed to stay out of the way of all the commuters leaving the city. They came in droves and were in a hurry. Finally, I found a McDonalds which meant a probable Wi Fi connection. It only had a small seating area, but I was able to find a place in the corner. I ate my sandwich, watched commuters buy food for their rides home, watched an employee mop the same spot multiple times, and then actually successfully posted my first day's pictures on Facebook. Unless I had talked to the people I would be visiting along the way I had not told most of my Facebook friends what I was doing. I wanted people to see a new picture every day from someplace different. As I went along people would recognize key landmarks and realize I was doing a bit of travel.

After eating dinner I had some time to kill. Several more hours. Every big station has a somewhat different way of showing departures. Chicago did not display the departure gates until 30 minutes before trains were scheduled to leave. I had no idea which track I would be leaving from. And there were a lot of tracks. So, I spent some time in the Great Hall reading. I had brought Dan Brown's book "Inferno". After getting bored reading I walked around some more. The commuters kept on coming. Another thing I found was that in the big, busy, city terminals there were lots of panhandlers. Some looked down-and-out and even pathetic. Others were a surprise. I am sitting around a small water feature under an escalator and a well-dressed lady came and sat by me. Her story was she had a job back in Memphis, where she was headed, but was short on cash to feed her kids before she got there. I never saw any kids with her but gave her $5. I did not budget for panhandlers and don't recall giving money to anyone else on the trip. Instead I tried my best to avoid them. They somehow could float just below the radar of the police and security in many of the busier stations.

Leg 2
September 9-10
#48 Lakeshore Limited
Chicago to Albany, NY   759 Miles   17:20 Hours
States: Illinois, Indiana, Ohio, Pennsylvania, New York

Most trains did not assign seats for their routes. Only on the busy east coast runs did I have an assigned seat. I also did on the LA to Portland run. However, you don't know what to expect regarding room. While still in Chicago I continued to hang out in the common areas until I wandered toward the gates about 45 minutes before my 9:00 train. I went through some gate doors and there was another very large waiting area I had not seen, specifically for my train. I had no idea it was there and wondered how all the people that were already there knew. A line had formed at the departure gate entrance. I was a ways back in line and kicked myself for not checking this out earlier. There were a couple of hundred people in the room, either in line ahead of me or waiting in seats. At 8:30 they started announcing boarding instructions. Where to go if you had a sleeper car, etc. Surprise. They said that senior passengers would board first. That would be me. So, to front of line I went. Also, there would not be seat assignments. I had a good chance for a window and good place to sleep.

Once out on the platform Amtrak personnel would direct us to cars based on destination. I was going to Boston. However, this train only went as far as Albany, New York. More on that connection later. As it turned out I got a seat on the left side of the train so I would not have morning sun. We would be leaving after dark and as soon as the train crossed the Indiana line we would lose an hour. At that point lights were turned down to low and everyone tried to sleep. During the night we would cross northern Indiana, northern Ohio, and make daylight by Erie, PA. Then across New York state with stops in Rochester, Syracuse, Utica, and Schenectady.

Trains east of Chicago are not double-deckers. The tunnels in the east (going into New York) were not big enough to accommodate the higher cars. Plus, much of the east coast were commuter trains. The seating of the single level cars were similar to the double decker cars. There were also sleeper cars and a dining car. However, you did not sit up as high for scenery.

In leaving I was interested in seeing what I could of the Chicago railyards. We went right next to the White Sox stadium (US Cellular Field), where a game was being played. I recognized the sights near Hammond, IN and onto Gary. I watched night go by until South Bend, IN when I tried to sleep. This would be my first night on a train. I knew from flying at night I usually did not do well sleeping. Even with two seats and the ability to recline I just can't sleep. I would listen to music on my I-pod for a while. They kept it cool at night. My jacket was my blanket.

I do recall a couple of nighttime stops. There are no announcements at night so if no one stirs to get up there is really nothing to wake anyone. Remember those tickets above your seat? Conductors would wake anyone if they had to get off at the next stop. I never saw anyone miss a stop. The ride is smooth, however, sometimes you do notice the absence of movement when at a station. I recall waking at Cleveland as it was still just getting light. I don't recall what I did for breakfast that morning. The trains did have a club car (snack bar) that included breakfast sandwiches, pastries and the like. I don't recall lunch either that day.

The train ran along some of the old Erie Canal once we were east of Buffalo, NY. I could see some of the old canal bed, but sights came up too fast for pictures. In fact, I didn't take any pictures that day until we broke down. (Yes, we were soon to break down). We passed through Utica which I recalled going through on a family vacation after leaving the Baseball Hall of Fame in Cooperstown, NY. That was probably 1990. We were due in Albany at 2:50pm where the Boston passengers would literally cross the platform and board the Boston train. That train was scheduled to arrive in Boston at 8:00 pm. My brother-in-law Bob would pick me up there and we would drive the 90 miles to Concord, NH where I would spent the weekend. However, near Little Falls, NY sometime after 1:00 the train made an emergency stop. We had been running parallel to a state highway and I had just seen a road sign indicating we were 76 miles from Albany. We were not going terribly fast, but you could tell the stop was not like any others we had along the way.

Amtrak does not tell its passengers a lot about what is going on in a situation like this. It was obvious that our stop was unusual and not expected. We got some apology from the crew and the conductor came through reassuring us the problem was being addressed. Most passengers wanted to know how this would impact making our connection in Albany. There was only 15 minutes between trains. We were told that the Albany/Boston train was basically a continuation of Amtrak 48 (the one we were on) so it would not leave until we arrived. Lots of people were going on to New Your City and they would stay on this train.

The information came to us slowly and much of it came from a fellow passenger who sat across the aisle from me. I had observed that he had sat up much of the night with a large electronic component (about the size of an old VCR). He had it resting on his pulldown tray and it was plugged into the electrical outlet. He had an ear piece to listen. I had no idea what it was. He looked to be about 50 and I would guess was the nerd type in school. He had not wanted to engage in any conversation with others around him. It turns out that the "VCR" was a CB radio. He could listen to the communication from the engine to Amtrak control. He did not so much as tell us, but we heard him (easily) broadcast our situation to his CB listeners. He related that a hose had come off some part of the locomotive. That was easily fixed, but the computer that was necessary to restart the engine would not allow a re-boot. The computer went through a checklist of safety items and it would not proceed. Amtrak was trying to talk the engineer through procedures, but they were not working. Eventually they decided to bring a circuit board for the computer out from Albany. That would be 76 miles by car and then the repair time. We would be here for a while.

"This is Amtrak 48, Amtrak 48, broke down in Little Falls, New York. Amtrak can't get the engine started and are bringing a new computer part from Albany. We are expecting a long delay". That was a typical announcement from our CB friend to his listeners (and all who could hear him in our car). He was perturbed and was more agitation with each broadcast. The conductor would come through, but not add much to what we had already heard. The power had been out for a short while, but we now did have power. Then they came through handing out snacks. Better than nothing. I used the time to take some inside pictures of our car, read, and catch up on the sleep I did not get the night before. Out of politeness I did not sneak a picture of Mr. CB. I should have.

Finally, Mr. CB stood up and started to address those around him. Not directly, but in a way that allowed me to answer him. He wanted to know why we were not more upset. Why weren't we doing something? Call Amtrak, or something. I'm not sure, but in our listening to him there may have been included a call into Amtrak itself. I asked what we could do that would speed up the repair. We knew a part was coming along with an IT person. These events were things that were outside of our control. We were warm and dry, could get food if we needed it and we had a comfortable place to sit. I have suffered through much worse delays on planes. A while later more information came from "Mr. CB". It seems he was now going to miss his appearance on the "Today Show" the next morning! Oh wow. Now this is around 3:30 in the afternoon and if we got going soon he would be in New York by 10:00pm. He had an earlier arrival time than the Boston train would have. However, that was only part of the issue with him. He needed his sleep (I don't think he slept much on the train), and he would not get enough sleep to be able to get up in time to make the show. I again pointed out that he would still have a good part of the night to sleep. He could be resting right now instead of fretting. Then someone asked if he should call the Today Show to advise his situation. Then we learned the whole nature of his trip. He was meeting up with some friends and they were going to wear their Chicago Cubs apparel and line up outside the studio like the hundreds of other people that do the same thing each morning! And he was going to miss his chance because he would not get enough sleep…. I regret not calling Connie and have her tape the show the next morning. I'll never know if he made it. With that knowledge everyone gave him a wide space and once the train got moving again (after 3 ½ hours) he did stay on the radio bemoaning his late arrival into New York to his listeners.

Just in front of Mr. CB was a man in his 40's wearing a ball cap saying, "Cold War Veteran". That intrigued me as in a sense we are all veterans of the Cold War. He had been in the Navy during a time when there were no wars for us to be involved with. It was after Viet Nam, but before the breakup of the Soviet Union. He was part of a "lobby group" trying to get some recognition for a memorial, or something, to give his service time some recognition. I was sorry I spoke to him. Thousands of men and women serve in our military during times of peace or are nowhere near any action. While tensions could be tight at times for the most part we lived at peace. His shining moment was ashore on liberty somewhere and in the same bar were some soviet sailors. Somehow, he survived the moment to tell about it.

No fights broke out, but if there had been he would have protected our counties honor. So, he (and apparently some others) feel they should be given recognition for their service. Enough said.

During our delay I had been in contact with brother-in-law Bob. He was able to get on the Amtrak website and get updated arrival times into Boston. They kept getting pushed back. In addition, to having a 90-minute drive each way for him this was the opening night of the NFL season and New England was playing. It was looking more and more like Bob would miss the game on TV, but have to listen on the radio. By the time we got to Albany our Boston arrival time was 11:00pm. Bob checked out hotel information, but the only thing near the train station ran over $300 for the night. Not an option.

Leg 3
September 10
#448 Lake Shore Limited
Albany NY to Boston   200 Miles   4:56 Hours
States: New York, Massachusetts

The wish was that we could make up some time after we left Albany. After crossing the Hudson it was very dark and for the most part I could not see anything from the train. I only knew we were moving very slowly, and it seemed we were switching tracks every few minutes. Towns of Springfield, Worchester, and Framingham were passed through with only some of the street lights to see. I would guess the rail beds here were very old with a lot of direction change options for freights, commuter trains, and the lowest priority - Amtrak. Instead we lost some more time and we rolled into Boston at 11:30pm. I had checked my bag in Chicago, which seemed like a good idea at the time, over 24 hours ago. However, I lucked out. As we walked by the baggage car toward the terminal, they were giving bags directly to passengers instead of taking them inside and making us wait. I grabbed my bag and found Bob waiting past the line of taxis and we were finally on our way to Concord. I had been traveling for only 2 days but was already tired from a night on the train and the anxiety of our delay.

Concord, New Hampshire Stay

We arrived at Bob and Robyn's house around 1:00am. Bob and Robyn live in Concord, New Hampshire, and have for about 30 years. I had not visited them since that family vacation in 1990. Coming into town at night the city seemed bigger than the last time I was there, but Bob said it really wasn't. I was shown to my room (niece Emily's, who now lives and works in Boston) and the bath and didn't take too long to get to sleep. Bob had to work the next day (until noon) and I was going to get up when I woke up. That turned out to be after 9:00.

When I came down in the morning Robyn was reading the paper and we had a chance to visit for the morning. We see Bob and Robyn and weddings and funerals, usually every couple of years. They came to Indiana for son John's wedding. I also met up with Bob and Emily in Chicago when I was there on business a few years ago. Emily was going to grad school there at the time. I noted that I had only been gone a little over 48 hours but had already passed through or been in nine states.

Bob came home in the early afternoon and we spent the afternoon driving around Concord. Their daughter Jennifer had just started a new position as a Dean at St. Paul's School, a very exclusive private high school in Concord. We drove around the campus and noted that freshman orientation was in progress. Jen lives on campus on housing provided by the school. She had stopped to visit us briefly in Minnesota in late July and I would see her again on Sunday. We drove around and saw more of the city. A farmer's market, state capitol, and houses they used to live in. After dinner we went to the movie "A Walk in the Woods" with Robert Redford and Nick Nolte. An unlikely pair who set out to walk the Appalachian Trail. Probably not a movie I would normally go see, but it did somewhat fit into our Saturday plans.

On Saturday Bob and I rose early and drove north to the White Mountains and took the Cog Train to the summit of Mt. Washington, (6,288 ft.). I have always heard about Mt. Washington. The highest winds ever recorded on earth were at the summit back in the 30's. (232 mph). While the mountain is not that high there has never been a recorded temperature of more than 74 degrees at the top.

There are three ways to the top of Mt. Washington. For hikers the Appalachian Trial crosses the summit as it does several peaks in the Presidential Range. Also, there is a toll road, however that would be no fun. Our way to the top was a 3 mile "cog" train that goes right up the face of the mountain. What is a cog train? Each locomotive (Made special for this route), has a center cog gear the uses a center rail to "gear up" the mountain. It is slow and steep and kind of fun. Much of the route is over 30 degrees of incline. The seats in the passenger cars are reclined to react to that angle. The rail bed does not look too secure with many of the ties and rails elevated above beds of rocks by jacks and the like. Several trains are on the mountain at any one time and there are side tracks so up and down trains can get by each other.

Once on top there is a weather station, observation area, and museum. All is built from the abundant rock at the summit. We were fortunate in having a nice morning. We could see over to Maine, Vermont, New York, and up into Canada. We had clear skies and not too windy. The Appalachian Trail is very rocky at the summit. Each step is from one big bolder to another. There were a lot of weekend hikers and most had poles (like ski poles) for balance. Bob had done this part of the trail with his daughters and even stayed at a hiker lodge as part of the experience. Something I would have liked to have done in younger days.

Weather can change very quickly at the summit and by the time we were having lunch at the Mt. Washington Hotel (Very beautiful) back down the mountain we watched the summit as it was slowly covered by clouds. I'm glad we did the trip early enough to be able to see the scenery. This was a very nice addition to my trip. One of several that I would have. It kept a rail theme for my adventure.

The rest of Saturday and Sunday was spent watching football and visiting. Sunday was a rain out so the local hike we had planned was scrubbed. A good day for rain and was only one of two total rain days of the entire trip. This was the opening weekend of the NFL season. I'd miss most of the next four weeks' worth of games. Or I thought I would.

Bob was now working right in Concord, but for many years he commuted by bus to Boston on Monday's to start his work week. Monday morning he put me on the 5:00am commuter bus that took me right to the Boston train station. The ride was about 90 minutes and I had plenty of time to make my 8:15 train to New York. The Boston station also doubles as the bus station and many commuters were coming into the city to work. Like many larger stations I found a McDonalds and then just tried to stay out of the way until it was time to board my train.

Leg 4
September 14
#171 Northeast Regional
Boston to New York City   231 Miles   4:05 Hours
States: Massachusetts, Rhode Island, Connecticut, New York

The Eastern Corridor is one of the several Amtrak routes that doubles as commuter runs. New York bound trains leave all day long from Boston. This was the only train that had Wi-Fi for my entire trip. Amtrak has tried using Wi-Fi all the way to Florida, but since it could not supply a steady signal to passengers it stopped the service. People that needed internet could use their own phone devise to get that service. This four-hour trip to New York was one of the more interesting from a scenery standpoint until I got to Texas. We went through Rhode Island and then along the Long Island Sound through Connecticut and into New York. I saw the towns of Mystic, New London, New Haven, and Bridgeport. Lots of nice homes and boat marinas. Something I found interesting was that no matter where I was in the country you could see where homeless people "camped" out along the rail line. Old mattresses, shopping carts, and litter could be seen in areas where the rail bed was not totally observable from the street. This was something I really was not expecting in what would be considered an affluent area.

I had been joined by a young college student. She was from Lithuania and had just finished her summer job of working at a five-star New England resort. Her school had already stated back home, but she would be able to join classes later. She and some friends were taking one additional week to see New York City and Washington DC. I found myself playing tour guide as we came into New York City from Queens. It was easy to pick out the Empire State Building, Chrysler Building, and even the new World Trade Tower in lower Manhattan. I was confused by one very tall apartment building that was closer to us than the others. I thought that the height was just a matter of perspective in that it was closer. However, I found out after I got back that it was the 432 Park Avenue Building. At almost 1,400 feet tall, it could be the tallest in the city if the tower of One World

Trade Center is not counted. The "tour guide" needs to keep up on the New York buildings. Miss Lithuania was very pleasant to talk with and her English was very good. She noted the book I was reading and had also read the Dan Brown books. I was not really into the book yet and thought it too much like "The Da Vinci Code" or "Angels and Demons". She reassured me that it would not continue that way.

New York City Layover

I am always amazed at the hustle and bustle of New York City. I had three hours between trains and decided to check my bag for the Florida train and go up and see the city. Basically, I just walked the distance around Madison Square Garden, which sits on top of Penn Station. I took pictures of the Empire State Building, Main Post Office Building and some street scenes. Under the station is a maze of hallways, shops, places to eat, and rail related services. The New York commuter lines make up most of the passengers and they were coming and going all afternoon. I found a Taco Bell where I was able to get Wi-Fi and post some pictures. Or at least I hoped I did. It would be my last internet connection until south Florida later the next day.

It is fun to watch people in these big train stations. One individual stood out in the area where I was waiting for the Florida train. He was probably in his 70's and had long white hair that was down to his shoulders. He had an Uncle Sam beard to match his hair. His attire was a material that I could not determine, but it gave the appearance of a buckskin suit with a shirt of matching color. He walked slowly as you would expect with age. And he had a hat that made him look like a Buffalo Bill want-a-be. However, what got me to notice him was that fact he held a notebook sized American Flag up to his chest as he walked. He just walked around saying nothing but getting a lot of looks and smiles. I did not hear him speak at that time. A few people snuck his picture and I wish I had. At the time I didn't realize he would be riding on the same train car that I would be on. But, by then a few other characters had my attention.

Leg 5
September 14-15
#97 Silver Meteor
New York to West Palm Beach, Florida   1,324 Miles   25:37 Hours
States: New York, New Jersey, Pennsylvania, Delaware, Maryland, Washington DC, Virginia, North Carolina, South Carolina, Georgia, Florida

The train out of New York City would go all the way to Miami, if I wanted to go that far. I was going as far as West Palm Beach. My ride would be about 24 hours and I would spend another night on the train. The eastern rail corridor must be complex. There are more passenger, commuter, and freight trains than one could imagine. I was interested in seeing how much scenery I could see. In leaving New York we would go under the Hudson River to New Jersey, through Philadelphia, a small bit of Delaware and then though Baltimore, and Washington DC. I had never actually been to downtown Philadelphia. However, views were not always good. I did not have a window seat, but was on the aisle on the right side of the train. Going into big cities the train is often underground so there is not too much to see. We reached Washington in early evening and it would get dark shortly after leaving that station. Amtrak, in the Northeast corridor, uses electric locomotives. At Washington DC we would be delayed about half an hour while they brought in a diesel locomotive for the rest of the trip. When leaving DC, I could see the Capitol with the recent scaffolding around the dome, the back of the Smithsonian, the Washington Monument and a lot of office buildings. Then over the Potomac to Alexandrea and then south though Virginia and into another night.

Expect for a few river crossings the views were disappointing in the east. The rail beds are old and well established. The railroad right-of-way is wide enough to allow the growth of a lot of trees between the tracks and whatever you would be interested in seeing. Also, the rail bed was somewhat lower than the normal ground level. Since we were not on double decker cars we were closer to the ground. With scenery lacking on the outside I focused on the people I was traveling with.

Unlike the routes I traveled through the west the Silver Meteor was not a train made up of tourists. I was a minority, in more ways than one. Many people were traveling to Florida, or somewhere in the south, by the only means of travel available to them. Their only other alternative would be the bus. However, the train provided much more room than a bus, provided meals, and had much larger lavatories than a bus would provide. I don't know the price difference, but the Amtrak fares were very reasonable for even longer rides.

My seat partner was named George. He was Mexican heritage, retired, and in is late 60's. He did not own a car. His home had been in New York City and he had a wife, children, and grandchildren all living there and spread out up and down the coast. However, because of health reasons he needed to live in Florida. George had an apartment in West Palm Beach where he could live nicely. His kids were grown and he could travel by train to see them. And he got back to New York frequently. Being a senior citizen I think a one-way ticket was well under $100 for him. He had everything he needed with him. All his food was in his bag, which consisted of sandwiches and water. He had done the trip many times and was helpful to me in pointing out some things. He turned out to be a very nice gentleman and we talked on-and-off a fair amount. He was interested in my trip and we talked about the sights I wanted to see. He had a cell phone and when talking to his family he spoke Spanish. However, his English was very good.

One row ahead of me on the opposite side of the aisle was the most diverse traveling companions I ran across. They were not traveling together, but through the luck of the draw were sitting together. The woman on the aisle was the librarian type. She had her knitting and books and looked like she was hoping for a nice relaxing trip down south. Her seat mate was a young black man. Not too long after we left New York the young man began the first of many long, animated phone conversations. He used the language of the ghetto in addressing someone who appeared to be the mother of his daughter. A daughter that he seemed to be concerned about. He was talking loud enough for probably the entire car to perfectly hear his side of the conversation. A normal exchange would be "I don't care about your "mother ****ing situation" or "don't "mother ****ing hang up on me". "What have you been doing to my "mother ****ing daughter?" "How many kids do you have anyway"? He was lecturing, reprimanding, being hung up on, threatening, and had much more colorful vocabulary that I just gave him credit for. Now imagine Ms. Librarian trying to read. She soon gave that up. Maybe she would knit. No one had the nerve the challenge this individual. No train personnel came through the car. Newer boarding passengers were not coming onto our car, which appeared to be full. One passenger came up and stood and stared at him for a minute but got no acknowledgement. He might be off the phone for a couple of minutes then start in again.

At some point he would talk to someone else. That conversation was almost civil and not laced with profanities. He seemed to be getting advice from that person and we learned a little more of his situation. I think he was going to meet the lady who was the subject of his tirades. While she was mother of his daughter, I don't think they were ever that close nor knew each other that well. There was a lot he did not know about her but had heard enough from others about whom she was hanging out with and the like. He realized it was a terrible situation for his "mother ****ing daughter". I almost felt sorry for him. This continued on and off for almost two hours. Ms. Librarian retreated to the club car. The seats were not as comfortable there, but she had some peace. Soon after dinner the phone calls ended.

There were many heavyset people riding this train. Some grossly overweight. The man in front of me had to be over 400 pounds. He was on oxygen and had a young man (son?) traveling with him. However, he took a good part of two seats. He reclined back in front of me, but as explained before that was not a problem. I saw him get up once to go to the lavatory and to bring food back from the club car. I didn't see anything healthy on his food tray. He had a shuffle when he walked, and a step was only a few inches at a time. Couple that with a moving train I was thankful he did not end up in someone's lap. He sat across from the librarian. I ate in the Dining Car. No reservations were needed and there was a fair amount of room. Like George, most of the people traveling on this train could not afford a $15 dinner. I sat opposite an obese black man who took up the entire side. He ordered a steak and enjoyed each bite thoroughly. (I enjoyed the half chicken with rice.) I told him about my trip, however, when he talked it was hard to understand him. He was somewhat soft spoken and I don't always hear well. I hate silence so tried a couple of topics of conversation. He talked some, and I swear he called me "son" when I left and he wished me well on my trip.

In their glory days, before airplanes, rail travel was the only way to go long distances. If you had a sleeper car you could change cloths easily and "dress" for dinner. While eating I did observe on older gentleman come in the from the sleeper car side of the dining car. He was dressed in a tie and dinner jacket and was ready to enjoy a find dining experience. NOT. I don't think he was even actually seated. I am guessing they took his meal to his cabin, which they were willing to do. It would have been interesting to hear his story. By not getting a sleeper I did get to experience a segment of society that I would not normally meet. I would have a couple of more days to experience the same before I headed west.

Each car had two large restrooms. One could accommodate wheel chairs. One concern about public restrooms is how prior visitors leave things for the next occupant. I always through that pee on the toilet seat was the result of a man not lifting it. Wrong. Seems there are women who probably squat over the seat so as not to touch it and then proceed to pee on the seat. They are too big to turnaround to look at their mess so just leave it that way. By directly following such women into the lav I finally have been able to change my opinion somewhat on wet toilet seats. Since we had almost a full train the train crew had a real challenge in keeping the lavatories clean. We would occasionally be directed to the next car as they unclogged a mess. Since I slept poorly, I was up very early and could spend time changing my shirt and brushing my teeth while things were somewhat clean from the night servicing. These restrooms had locks on the doors, but for many first-time users they could not figure out how to lock the sliding door from inside. If locked, a light would be on outside showing the room was occupied. I only walked in on one woman who had not locked the door. She was squatted over the seat. "Excuse me". She did not seem bothered by the interruption when she exited as I showed her how to use the lock.

Meanwhile, Buffalo Bill had trouble sleeping as well. I found him sitting with a somewhat dazed look in the club car as I passed though for breakfast. He had been in my car, but farther back. The flag was gone by now. He got off sometime in the morning. I had missed most of the south to the darkness. Finally, we had a new day around Savanah, Georgia.

I sat through most of Florida talking with George and looking at whatever we could see between trees. As usual I probably got about three hours of sleep, so I had breakfast as soon as the dining car was open at 6:30. It was surprising at the number of cattle ranches in Florida. I mentioned my friend Jeff drove a cattle truck to Texas for slaughter, sometimes weekly. Then the fruit. From the train it was hard to tell oranges from other fruits, but they were plentiful.

We had a stop in Jacksonville and then a lot of people got off in Orlando, as I would two days later on my way back north. About every three hours the trains do an extended stop to allow smokers to get their fix. It also gives passengers a chance to get out and walk off any stiffness. Jacksonville and Orlando had smoke break times.

There were two instances on the trains where passengers snuck a smoke in the lavatory. There was a man in his 30's who boarded our car and apparently had not had his tobacco fix before he got on. We had a smoke stop coming up soon, but he could not wait. The Conductors can smell tobacco smoke two cars away. As soon as this guy sat down from a restroom visit there was an announcement "Smoking is not allowed anywhere on Amtrak trains. Anyone caught smoking will be escorted from the train at the next station." I was told that not only that, but they are escorted totally from the station property and local authorities are notified. There is then a lifetime ban from any further Amtrak travel. The person I mentioned was not caught. He somehow made it through the night, but was first off the train at every smoke break.

South Florida Stay

I said good-bye to George as we rolled into West Palm Beach pretty much on schedule. To meet me were a few of the newest Florida citizens. Connie's sisters Debbie and Patty and Patty's husband Jim. Debbie had moved there from Seattle after her divorce and picked the area close to where Patty and Jim were going to retire. Patty and Jim had just arrived from Boston and were house hunting. We all stayed at Debbie's apartment. I had the air mattress on the living room floor. However, that was a joy after a night on the train. I always slept well after a night on the train. Patty and Jim had vacationed there quite often before picking this as a retirement area. They knew their way around fairly well. We found a place to eat called "Shrimpers" in Stuart. Even being tired it was nice to sit up and talk to family. I had just left their brother Bob the day before, so we were all up to date on all the family news. We would all meet up again in a few weeks in Virginia for the wedding. (The bride was their brother Jims' daughter).

Wednesday the 16th saw four inches of rain in southern Florida. After sleeping in and having breakfast we did venture out. I wanted to get a good picture of the ocean, without getting soaked, to post on-line. We finally found a covered pavilion at the end of a jetty where I was able to get some pictures. We then had lunch at Flannigan's, also in the Stuart area. Dinner at Deb's, more talking, and a debate on TV, and back to my air mattress. It was a short visit.

Leg 6
September 17
#98 Silver Meteor
West Palm Beach to Orlando   200 Miles   3:36 Hours
State: Florida

The rain had mostly stopped the next morning and I was heading back north to Orlando after donuts for breakfast. Deb found the way to the West Palm station on her own. The train left the station around 9:45 and arrived in Orlando at 1:20. So a short ride. I sat next to a guy who I named "Walmart Man". He worked for Walmart and proceeded to tell me about issues with kids and seeing them and how he needed to travel by train, etc. More information than I needed to know. He was only on the train for a while and I wished him well. The remaining clientele mirrored what I had seen coming down the coast. With everything on time this was probably the least memorable leg of my entire trip. By this time I was no longer checking bags. There was always plenty of storage space above the seats, so it made exit from the train quick. My bags were not that heavy or bulky, so I never had problems in stowing bags. I did not eat on the train as Jeff and I had planned on going out once I arrived at his place.

Port Canaveral, Florida Stay

Jeff had his pickup across the street from the station (apparently the same place he had parked the month before when he wondered where I was), and after we figured out how to get out of town we were on our way to Coco Breach. Jeff and I worked together for Continental Insurance on and off between 1975 and 1986. He then finished his working career with Intel in Folsom, CA. He retired in 2007 and bought a used 46-foot sailboat near Coco Beach and lived on the boat in a marina at Port Canaveral. He is just across from where the cruise ships depart daily. I visited him there twice before in 2008 and 2009. His boat, the Wayward Wind, kind of turned out be to a lemon and he was always running into hardware or mechanical issues when attempting to sail. So instead of seeing the seven seas he spent much of his time in the marina. In fact, he spent almost all his time in the marina. From friends he made there he had picked up a truck driving job. They take a load of cattle from Florida nonstop to Texas. Then turn around and deadhead back. Jeff is on-again, off-again with this outfit. He had just gotten in the night before and crashed at a friend's place. He had not even been back to his boat before picking me up.

The boat looked older (needed paint) and inside had more clutter than the last time I visited. People accumulate stuff no matter where they live and there is limited space on a boat to stow stuff. What had previously been my bunk at the stern was now a catchall full of "stuff". It is always good to see Jeff. We usually don't agree politically, but we go back over 40 years and have a lot of common work and personal experiences. We went to a late lunch at "Fish Lips" a favorite of his from my 2008 visit. Then we went to the movie "Everest". I had not planned on seeing movies on this trip but was now at my second one. Then a late dinner at "Steak N Shake". Usually can't go wrong there. It was already a week since my late arrival in Boston and I watched Thursday Night Football with Denver and KC before I retired. My bed was the bench seat in the main cabin. It could be made up with sheets and blanket and was almost long enough for me. Not a great sleep as any time I needed to turn over I lost my covers. Plus going to the lavatory at night was always fun on this boat. I had to go to mid-boat and try not to disturb Jeff, whose bedroom was the front half of the boat. To flush the toilet was a noisy hand pump with a loud suction sound as the waste went somewhere below.

One neat thing about mornings in the marina was that when you looked out there was always a couple of huge cruise ships that had come in quietly during the night. Sometimes I would wake to hearing their PA systems giving passengers disembark instructions. The boats would sit there all day and leave in the late afternoon. Sometimes as many as three would be in port at one time. My favorite were the Disney boats as they played the theme from "When You Wish upon a Star" through their horns as they left port. We had bagels for breakfast and I did my laundry as Jeff had a doctor appointment. I had just done laundry the prior Sunday but would not have a chance again until I reached Oregon in about a week.

Jeff always has friends from the marina. Most don't live there but hang out there on their boats a lot. We met Jim and Nancy for lunch. I think I had met them on my last visit as Nancy is friendly and I recall her hanging out on the finger pier of the marina with a friend enjoying a drink. A lot of New York culture makes it to Florida, including the style of pizza the restaurant served. You could buy by the slice and it made a meal. From there we revisited the Coco Beach Pier. It was not the best day, but there were still a fair number of people on the beach for a mid-September Friday. The marina has shower facilities for the boat owners and guests. I would not get a shower again until late Monday in New Orleans, so I took advantage of that.

Dinner with more friends. We had Mexican with Bob and his new fiancé, whose name escapes me as she is Russian. Seems her American husband had recently died and she was left with no knowledge of their finances or how to dispose of their boat. A financial adviser had been working with her, but when she shared her plans with Jeff he realized she was going to be ripped off by thousands of dollars on the boat. The "advisor" was also a boat broker and was only interested in own profit. Ms. Russian had been taught to trust no one, but Jeff and Bob were able to get her to back out of the deal and they helped her sell the boat. With their new trust she became engaged to Bob. They had fun with her as she was still very naïve regarding many things American.

Back at the marina we went into the "Club Room". There was a pool table, foosball, and a big screen TV. A man and his son were watching TV, but we soon turned to the baseball playoffs. Then a man came in who Jeff knew fairly well. The man's son worked for the marina. We started talking baseball and the man (older than me) said he played in the White Sox organization when he was young and got to hang out with the likes of Nellie Fox and Luis Aparicio in Spring Training back around 1960. The White Sox played in the 1959 World Series, which was the first series I recall watching and still knew some players names. He wanted to share with me a book he had recently written and went to get a copy. His name was Lathan Hudson. I expected the book to be about baseball, but it seems Mr. Hudson was a country western songwriter in Nashville for many years and the book was his recollection about many of the stars he got to know. I mentioned Branson, Missouri, and he wanted my opinion on that scene. A very interesting man to meet and talk with. I had to go back to the boat to get a pen so he could sign the book. "Bruce, great talking to you about sports and the like. Have fun on your trip. Best – Lathan Hudson". Then verbally he added "Yeah Obama gets on his prayer rug five times a day and prays to the east". OK. With that I wished him a good evening.

Leg 7
September 19-20
#98 Silver Meteor
Orlando to Washington DC   899 Miles   17:22 Hours
States: Florida, Georgia, South Carolina, North Carolina, Virginia,
Washington DC

To get to Los Angeles Amtrak used to go from Orlando, through New Orleans, and continue all the way to Los Angeles. I have heard two reasons why the Orlando to New Orleans run had been discontinued. One was Hurricane Katrina and destroyed some of the rail lines and they had yet to be repaired. The other thing was that Amtrak was not able to come to any contractual agreement with the owner of that route to allow their trains to operate. Regardless, I had to back track all the way to Washington DC in order to then head southwest toward New Orleans. Based on train schedules this cost me several days' worth of time and some money. So, I reboarded the Silver Meteor north bound toward Washington. I would be spending another night on the train. My seat passenger was a very kindly black gentleman who was nice to talk with. He was older and I don't recall much else about him. He got off in Jacksonville, so I had both seats to myself for the night travel. I had a hot dog from the club car and bought some wine for later. (Don't ask which wine goes best with hot dogs). The night was not memorable except I slept poorly again. It was dark by Savanah, Georgia and we arrived in DC at 7:00 in the morning. This was not a sightseeing leg. It was a Sunday morning in DC. My train to New Orleans (The Crescent) would not leave until 6:30 that evening. I had almost 12 hours to tour the Capitol.

Washington DC Layover

I had been to Washington twice before. Once on a family vacation and another on business. I had seen most of the major monuments. I had been to the top of the Washington Monument and toured two of the Smithsonian Museums. As a family we were able to sit in the House Gallery while some debate was going on. I was planning to see the Mall area on foot and then use the Metro to go over to Arlington. I ate an early breakfast at the McDonalds in Union Station and used the Wi Fi to check my email, etc. I had Wi Fi on Jeff's boat by using the signal from his phone, so I was mostly up to date. After breakfast I found a bag check that would keep my bag for the day for $20. I didn't have to worry about lugging in around DC. Since 9-11 there is no longer the option of storage lockers for bags for security reasons. A real bag check is your only option.

I did check out the Metro Station just to make sure I knew where it was in relation to the depot so if I returned by subway I knew where I would come out. I got my bearings and set out walking. My first stop was the US Capitol, about 5 blocks away. At that hour of a Sunday morning the only other people out were runners and joggers. Most runners were in their late 20's and they were all serious about their efforts. The front of the Capitol was almost deserted. You can see from my pictures that only a few security personnel were present. I located the Supreme Court Building and the Library of Congress which face the Capitol. There were a couple of other tourists on the east side and one took my picture standing on the Capitol steps. I'm the only one there. Felt in charge.

Now I started my hike. I had my back pack on my back. All my travel stuff that was not in my suitcase was with me. The weather was cool, yet humid. It did not take me long to work up a sweat as I headed down the Mall. Distances are deceiving here. It is probably two miles to the Lincoln Memorial. The World War II Memorial, Washington Monument, and White House are about half way, or a mile. While walking I passed the Smithsonian buildings on my left.

Before I left on my trip I had been working out at the local YMCA and was able to cover two miles walking in under 30 minutes. However, I felt I was already suffering from the inactivity of sitting on trains. This walk was going to be a real effort. Once I approached the

118

World War II Memorial I was tired, and my shirt back was soaked through. I had to rethink my walking plans. I had new shoes and one toe on my right foot was hurting and I ended up almost losing that nail before the day was done. The Mall in front of the museums was under a major renovation and there was a lot of sections where you could only go along the sidewalks. Also, as I got further down I saw that there was a major activity going on. There was a "run" for some charity as well as a big "revival tent" where a band was being set up and people were trying to entice people to come and worship with them. Not too many takers there as everyone was there for the running activity. Kids were with one parent waiting for the other parent to finish the race. At the finish line they all got goodie bags and I was caught up in a sea of runners and supporters. I finally got close to the Washington Monument and took some pictures and then a couple of the White House in the other direction. The World War II Memorial would be as far as I could go before I turned back to the Smithsonian.

I had not been to the World War II Memorial. It was built after my last visit. However, we did submit bios of my father and father-in-law while it was being built. After walking around the Memorial I found a kiosk that had computer terminals to look up veterans of the War. I found both my dad and father-in-law and was surprised to see my name as the contributor of the information. Then I had a personal disaster. I dropped my Canon camera while switching hands and it broke. It would not turn on and I was out of luck in figuring out how to fix it. That was a $1000 camera when first purchased in 2005. I had a backup, but that was my tablet which is cumbersome to use and I was only using it to post a few pictures on Facebook. My plan was to only use it for a couple of shots a day. I would have to rethink how I documented my trip with pictures.

I was also very tired of walking by this point. I am not sure how far I had walked, but the combination of being train bound, lack of sleep, sore feet, and a humid day took its toll on me. I stopped to rest often. I wanted to revisit the Air and Space Museum. I now walked back up the other side of the Mall in that direction. It was only 10:30 and I felt my blood sugar was getting low. I need to sit a while and eat, hydrate, and rest my feet. Finally, I made the Museum and lunch was already being serviced at the ultra-modern McDonalds inside. I still had most of my day left and really wanted to see Arlington and the Marine Corp Memorial. I would find the closest Metro station and take the train there. After resting a while and spending some time in the museum it was back out to the Mall and walk another half mile to the closest train station.

The entrance to Arlington is not that far across the Potomac, so the ride was short. Once up out of the Metro I just followed people to the main cemetery entrance to get my tour ticket. It looked like the wait could be up to an hour as there were several large tour groups getting ready to take the tours. However, I must have blended into one of the groups as they were people my age and I was on a tram shortly. Sneaky.

The Arlington tour makes multiple stops and you can get off the tram at any one. Then just catch the next tram to continue your tour. Most people want to see the Kennedy grave site. I took some pictures with my tablet and then looked at the view from the gravesite. Kennedy had visited the cemetery before he died and had commented that the view looking back to the city was beautiful. The trees may be covering more view now, but you have a straight-line view over the Lincoln Memorial towards the Capitol and Washington Monument. In reboarding the tram a lady fell and cut up her hand bad, plus other cuts and bruises. Everything stopped so they could give her medical attention. She appeared more embarrassed than hurt, however, when I did see her hands it was obvious, she needed more than simple first aid. The staff present looked like they were putting on rubber gloves for the first time and were not totally aware of what the medical kits contained. They finally decided to take her somewhere for further attention and we continued after about a 15-minute delay. I should note that over 100 people could ride on one of the trams.

I did not get off at any additional stops until the Marine Memorial. I was too tired and still frustrated that I broke my camera. After going down a long hill the tram stopped and the driver pointed in a general direction toward the Memorial and said, "that way". You could not see it from the drop-off site. Again, I started out walking with a few other people and it eventually came into view. I found seeing the Memorial was an emotional experience for me. My dad was injured on Iwo Jima and while he did not see the actual moment of the flag rising he did see it afterwards on the mountain top before he was injured. I had a difficult time talking to the Park Service employee who was there to answer questions and the like.

Okay, I had seen what I wanted to see and was time to make my way back to Union Station. The wait for a tram was very long. They must have really backed up somewhere along the line. I struck up conversation with a lady from Mission Viejo, California. I had lived there from 1981 to 1983 and we talked about the city and how much it had probably changed. She was with her daughter, son-in-law (military) and grandkids who were in a stroller. There was very limited room on the next tram and I was only able to board as I was a single.

Back at the Metro Station I had just missed a train and it would be upwards to 20 minutes before the next train going in the direction of the city came through. The platform was filling up with other Arlington tourists. My Mission Viejo friend showed up with her family and she was pleased she had not missed a train after getting held up in the cemetery. They were now going to try to go up the Washington Monument. I had to transfer trains and finally made it back to Union Station. I still had almost two hours before my New Orleans train. I went back to the McDonalds and a Wi Fi connection. Seating was limited as they were putting up new wall covering. Something they probably planned for a Sunday. I sat with a lady and updated my Facebook page with a few pictures and listened in on conversations. There was one couple who I saw there who not only ended up on the New Orleans train, but I saw again in the dome car heading for Los Angeles three days later. It can be a small world for some travelers.

Then there was the matter of my broken camera. I called Connie and asked if our son Dan could find a cheap replacement on Amazon. Dan was always finding things that replaced items we lost or broke. It might be a charger for a cell phone or a laptop battery. He was able to find a used Canon cameral body for $200. It would be compatible with my lenses and he could have it shipped so I would have it while still on my trip. We decided to have it shipped to my brother in Seattle. I would be there in about 9-10 days. I would have to do without a good camera until then, I would have the replacement in time to see Seattle and do the northern route through Glacier National Park and the Rockies.

Leg 8
September 20-21
#19 Crescent
Washington to New Orleans   1,152 Miles   26:07 Hours
States: Washington DC, Virginia, North Carolina, South Carolina, Georgia, Alabama, Mississippi, Louisiana

The train to New Orleans would be another night ride. I priced sleeping cars and it would be about $500 additional for me to upgrade at this time. After spending the prior night on a train, and two nights before that on the bench seat of a sailboat I looked forward to one more night of little sleep. We needed seat assignments and I was unable to get a window. My seat companion was a stuck-up blond in her 30's. She was not interested in conversation and just did her own thing. I did not see her interact with anyone. My one attempt at conversation was not welcomed so that was that. That reaction from her was the exception to normal friendly people. This would be a 26-hour ride. The Crescent left at 6:30 pm and it was soon dark. It was not light again until Gainesville, GA. We made Atlanta by 8:15am and were not scheduled to arrive in New Orleans until 7:32pm. In Alabama we crossed over to Central Time. We went through Birmingham, Tuscaloosa, and many other southern Alabama and Mississippi towns. I had not been through that part of the south, so the scenery was new to me.

Over the night and after Atlanta some seats opened up and I moved across the aisle to a window seat leaving the stuck-up blond to her own space. Not even a "thanks". I would have my own two seats for the rest of the trip. I probably slept better doing short naps than I did at night. I did my usual dining car breakfast and was seated with a very prim and proper older lady who had come from a sleeper car. She had done her make up for breakfast and fit the mold of the travelers of yore I had mentioned previously. She could not believe that someone of my position (whatever that was) would travel coach (like "coach" was a bad word), when fine accommodations were awaiting in a sleeper car. I explained the duration of my trip and the fact that I would have a sleeper on my next leg from New Orleans to Los Angeles. I appreciated her concern for my wellbeing. She was not wrong, but she was not underwriting my trip either. I spent the rest of the day watching scenery and was even able to use both sides of the train to take pictures as more seats opened up.

As we got closer to Louisiana you could still see Hurricane Katrina damage. Rows of no longer used FEMA trailers were seen in some places. In Slidell, LA you could see block after block of the city where the only thing left were cement driveways and sidewalks. No houses or any structure above ground level. The Katrina storm surge off Lake Pontchartrain wiped out whole portions of the city and nothing had been rebuilt.

Then we reached Lake Pontchartrain. I was not prepared for the size of this lake. We could not see across it. The rail line was on a rock and gravel bed elevated above the lake by about 10 feet. Running parallel to the rain line was an elevated highway. This was extra special as the sun was going down and it was nice getting sunset pictures over the lake. At one point we were delayed and sat for about half an hour as freight trains ahead of us had to clear out of the way.

New Orleans Layover

So, we finally made it across the lake into New Orleans, about 45 minutes late. If I had known my way around better I would have taken a streetcar to the hotel. "A Street Car Named 'Desire'" made these rounds at one time. Instead I took a taxi for about $10 and got to my Marriott Residence Inn near the French Quarter. I was wiped out. I found the Popeye's Chicken I had eaten when Connie and I attended a convention there in 2003. On TV was Monday Night Football with the Colts. I finished reading the "Inferno" and had a very good seven hours sleep. Boy was I tired.

New Orleans is a party town. It is the home of Mardi Gras. The French Quarter was described by me in 2003 as "enthralling decadence". In talking to the doorman of the hotel I said I had been here before. He immediately stated, "so this time you came without your wife". I said that was true, but I had a whole day to rest and I really needed the rest. The New Orleans to Los Angeles train, the Sunset Limited, is one of the few runs that is not daily. It departs New Orleans going west just three days a week. I arrived on a Monday evening and had to wait until Wednesday morning for the next train. While I did not like having to spend two nights in a hotel (the only hotel nights of my trip), I welcomed the rest. In leaving New Orleans I would be on a train for 3 ½ days until I reached Portland, Oregon. When I heard my cousin Mickey was not in Oakland I had to extend the next leg out of LA another 17 hours (and another night) on the train to make Portland. I would have three straight nights on a train, two would be a sleeper car and the next night from LA to Portland I was back in coach. In pricing the upgrade for a sleeper for the third night I got the same $500 price tag that I was offered for Washington to New Orleans.

I had breakfast at the Bistro at the hotel. It was nice to have a lazy morning not have to go out. However, I realized that I had some chaffing in some sensitive areas from all the walking I had done in DC. I bought some ointment at the drug store and some wine for the train. When you stay in a sleeper you can bring your own booze. So, I decided to pack away a couple of bottles of White Merlot. I then walked around the French Quarter. Not too much going on in the late morning. It was a nice day and I was looking for a restaurant I had eaten at when we were there before. It was on the second floor, but I could not find it without recalling the name. I was planning on coming back over for lunch or dinner later in the day. I then went back to my hotel and had a two-hour nap. I never take naps that long, so I knew I was catching up on needed sleep.

After the nap I decided to go back to the French Quarter. It was basically across Canal St. from where I was staying so pretty convenient. I also took my tablet to take some pictures. I found a courtyard restaurant and ordered a beer and some gumbo. One of my best trip pictures was of my bowl of gumbo. I posted that plus a couple of other shots of the French Quarter when I got back to my room. I did not venture out again. I had dinner at the hotel Bistro and spent the evening watching TV and repacking. I had about 3000 miles of train travel before I would unpack again. Since I would have a sleeper car for two nights I didn't have to worry about keeping some clothes in my knapsack. It would be a nice way to travel.

Wednesday morning had me up at 6:30 for the 9:00am #1 Sunset Limited. All the way to Los Angeles. Since it would be Pacific Time when I arrived the scheduled time on the train was about 47 hours. We would cover 2,000 miles. I took a cab back to the train station. The only food available in the depot was a Subway. The security screens for the restaurant were not even pulled all the way back yet, but they were open. The New Orleans depot does not double as a commuter train station. The Amtrak traffic was about all they had to cater to. All stations are different in how they organize passengers. New Orleans had a private room with nice seats for the sleeper car travelers. They came and got us when it was time to board. Your sleeper compartment was reserved so there would be no problem in getting a desirable seat.

Leg 9
#1 Sunset Limited
September 23-25
New Orleans to Los Angeles   1,995 Miles   46:35 Hours
States: Louisiana, Texas, New Mexico, Arizona, California

Once in my private compartment I was content. The "roomette" was not big. It had two bench seats facing each other. They would fold down to make the bed. Then a mattress with sheets would come down from the upper berth and go over the seats. The rooms could sleep two. There was a "pull down" berth above where a second person would sleep. It would have been very tight with two people. I was glad it was just me. If Connie and I do travel by train I will get one of the larger rooms. These cars were double-deckers and I was on the top level. There were 10 sleeping compartments on this end of the car with the aisle going down the middle. My view would only be out one side of the car. I was on the port (left) side. That was not good for pictures, but probably was the better side for scenery. The stairs to the lower level were in the middle of the car. On the opposite end of the second level were the larger rooms. There the aisle went down the window side of the car, for the compartments were twice as wide as my roomette. We had one toilet in our end of the car, but downstairs were a couple of more toilets and a shower room. There were also several more sleeping rooms on the lower level. At the ends of the lower levels were rooms that took the whole width of the car. I think the conductors shared one of those if no passengers booked them. You would have a couple of adults with kids in these rooms and they had their own toilet.

The rail cars seemed very well built. They were modeled after some of the trains in Europe and were designed to withstand use and yet have nice features. The double decker trains had an observation car with the glass rounded dome. The dining car was close. It was placed between the sleeper cars and the coach cars. All movement between cars was at the upper level. The doors opened easily and if you had your hands full (like food from the club car), you could use a kick plate to open the doors. It was fun watching new riders figure out the doors. At the lower level of the observation car was the club car. That was open most of the trip and they had a decent menu of quick food items and snacks. Also, beer and wine. Since we got our meals

126

included in the sleeper cars I would only use the club car for a mid-afternoon snack or for something to munch on in the evening.

By this time I had confirmation that my camera would be delivered to my brother's house in Seattle this week. I also realized that I could take still pictures with my video camera. I had never used it for that, but occasionally I would accidently have the camera in a "photo" mode and take pictures instead of video. I played around with it a little more to make sure I knew how it worked. Now I had my video camera and tablet. I would not know until I got back and got all the pictures loaded onto my computer that the video camera did not take good, high resolution, pictures. In fact, the pictures were disappointing. When shooting video the resolution is in high definition. But, not the photos. Since I was still wanting to post photos on line I was still taking some shots with my tablet. Those turned out being better pictures.

In leaving New Orleans I decided to start in the observation car. I knew we soon crossed the Mississippi and I didn't want to be limited to just one side of the train for a view. Not many folks were up there when we left. I was rewarded with very nice view as we crossed the Huey P. Long Bridge over the river and could see the city back in the distance. After a time I settled into my nice private room and only ventured out when I knew something was coming up that was on the right side of the train. I also got my travel "mind-set" back. The east coast travel was a challenge. Three nights in a coach car, weird people, and really a lack of scenery. Now I was able to reflect on why I wanted to do this trip in the first place. To relax and see the country. Not flying over or driving through but sitting back and enjoying. And I would have two days to relax in doing so. A sleeper car on the upper deck all the way to LA was the way to travel.

The Sunset Limited out of New Orleans stayed close to the Gulf Coast or the Intercostal Waterway. Much of the scenery was made up of all the supporting industry for the off-shore oil platforms. Lots of cranes, and pipes and yards where much of the gear was assembled or staged to take out to the Gulf. We ran parallel to the old US highway 90. In fact, we would be close to this road all the way across Texas. Lots of bayous. Bayou Lafourche, Bayou Blue, and Bayou Boeuf were all crossed before we got to Lafayette. You could still see areas damaged by Katrina. However, most of the mess had been cleared after 10 years.

Even though we would be on the train for almost two full days we only would have five meals in the dining car. We had missed breakfast the first day out and got into Los Angeles before breakfast would be served the third day. For lunch I had a hamburger in the dining car. I sat with some guys from Lodi, California. They were heading home after driving with a buddy to help his family move. The move included leaving them their car. His return fare on coach was reasonable enough that he was going to enjoy the trip. Lodi is south of Sacramento by about 40 miles. I had traveled there often when I worked in Sacramento, however, I had not been there in over 30 years. He was impressed that I knew where he lived and we talked about some of the other towns in that area and the valley in general as well as the drought.

There were some friendly folks on this train. Over a steak dinner I met Jeff Padgent and his wife Candy. They were going as far as San Antonio to see a college football game that weekend. One of their relatives was a coach and they tried to follow the team when they could. Sorry, I do not recall the teams as all the Texas teams run together for me. However, it was a Division I school. Jeff had the type of personality that he wanted to be your immediate best friend. He was very interested in my trip and I mentioned how I posted my progress on Facebook and watched the reactions of friends who did not know the scope of my trip. I was not surprised when I got to Los Angeles and I had a "friend request" from Jeff. I also had a chance to talk to people in the dome car. Jeff would be there as well as a couple from England who I will tell more about later. One thing I can say is that the type of people you meet from the sleeper cars was considerably different from those we met in coach going up and down the east coast.

We had almost half an hour in Houston. The sun was very low when we came into the city and I got some nice shots of the sun reflecting off the buildings. It was one of the stops where I got out to stretch my legs and try to get better pictures with both cameras. I should mention that coming into Houston the oil industry hardware continued as a common view. There were miles of storage yards of pipe. Big sections of pipe that when stretched out would go for miles. Also, Houston has a big rail yard with big switching areas that were busy with freight trains.

The Sunset Limited is really a "limited". There are only 20 stops between New Orleans and LA. That is over 100 miles between each station. In some cases we would go hours between stops. For example, the next stop after Houston was San Antonio. That was 210 miles and almost 5 hours. Tough luck for the smokers.

After dinner (steak) and leaving Houston I settled in to watch darkness descend over Texas. I had my I-pod and a bottle of wine. The porter is on board with us the entire trip and he needs to sleep as well. He was hoping to turn everyone's beds down somewhat early. I asked to be last, around 10:00. We were due to arrive in San Antonio at midnight and would be there almost 3 hours as Amtrak combined our train with the Texas Eagle coming down from Chicago. As it turned out those three hours were the best sleep I got. My berth was over the wheels at the back end of our car. It was not a smooth ride at that location. Trains switch tracks a lot. Every time we went over a switch I was tossed a bit. I could hear and feel the front of the car do the jog that comes with switching tracks. I then waited a couple of seconds and I was jolted as the rear wheels crossed the switch. Sometimes there was even a "bang" associated with the switch as metal was hitting metal somewhere below me. It was not the peaceful "clickety-clack" that I expected to rock me to sleep.

So how was the bed? Once the seats were folded down I threw my bag on the upper berth. With the bed down there was very little room between the bed and the closed door. The door was a sliding door. I could sit on the side of the bed and barely stand in the free space. In that area I left my slippers and pants so if I had to get up at night (and I always did) I could get something on quickly before going into the hall. I also had my clothes for the next day in another pile. If there had been two of us in the roomette it would have been a real challenge. Just to climb to the top berth meant going up steps build into the corner of the car. The steps doubled as shelves to put books, cell phones, cameras, and the like. Once up above there was not a lot of room between the bed and the top of the car. On top of that the air conditioning for the room was in the ceiling so if you were on top you had the blowing air to contend with. I did see several couples share these rooms. I don't think they slept well. I especially felt sorry for an elderly couple who shared a roomette. While two people could sleep together on the lower berth it would be cozy and no room to roll over unless done as a team. I would never travel with my wife using a smaller roomette. Rolling over eventually meant that the sheet did not follow so it was necessary to reorganize your bedding at night. All the looking forward to having a sleeping car did not mean I slept like a baby. I was up early. The next night had other challenges which I will explain later.

During the ride there are frequent announcements by the conductors and dining car staff. We are given several notices of the next station and if that stop will be a smoke break or not. The second day out we would have "smoke breaks" at Alpine, El Paso, and Tucson. There were often crew changes at these stops and a lot of folks got off just to stretch their legs. Other announcements were from the dining car. On the longer trains it was necessary to reserve an eating time for lunch and dinner. The staff could turn diners around in 30 to 45 minutes. Food had to be somewhat pre-prepared in the kitchen on the lower level. A dumbwaiter brought the food up to the servicing staff. Dinner dining times might start as early as 5:30 and could continue through 7:30. So there were frequent announcements as meals progressed. Earlier in the day the staff came to each berth and seat to ask for reservation preferences. Then they would call you to the dining car as each time came up. There was really no space to stand and wait so they tried to use the PA system to have people come to meals when space cleared out from the prior group.

There was an alternative to the dining car. The club car (located in the lower level of the dome car) had a lot of choices. On this run John ran the club car and he kept the entire train entertained with his announcements. If the dining car was running behind a bit he would come on and say "There is no wait for food at the club car. Come down and check us out. You can get pizza, burgers, sandwiches and all the fixings. Want your favorite beer or other spirits? Come down and pay me a visit" He created his own personal battle with the dining car as if he was in completion with them. His "one-up-man-ship" was often humorous. He would talk about the endless landscape of Texas, how the poor people flying right now were missing all the fabulous scenery and he would go into great detail as to the quality of his bagel's and toppings. The best was the next morning when many people were still sleeping. I was sitting on the john (yes, the PA went into there as well), and I heard a whispering, subliminal voice talking slowly. "Good morning. I don't want to disturb you if you are still resting. You must be in need of some nice warm coffee and a muffin. Get a head start on the dining car patrons and come down to the club car. I have breakfast sandwiches, rolls, coffee, and juice". Then he would whisper just single words. "Coffee". "Bagels". "Yogurt". "Cereal". He made me smile and

I did visit him a couple of times for snacks on the trip. No other route had this type of a character as staff on the train.

Of course, I got a free breakfast, so I ate very early then went to the dome car to watch sunrise over the Texas landscape. In the dome car I met up for about the third time with the couple from the Washington Union Station McDonalds, and who sat near me on the train as we came into New Orleans and now were on the LA train. The woman was very interested in my "USA by Rail" book that would describe the sights as they came up. I always had that with me in the dome car.

Prior to this trip I had been to Texas multiple times, but had always flown there. My longest drive was that between Austin and San Antonio. I had been to Dallas, Houston, San Antonio, Austin, and Midland-Odessa. I was really enjoying getting a feel of the big state from ground level. It is literally miles of prairie, grasslands, small mountain ranges, and a view that go for miles. You could see an occasional deer, cattle, and goats. Across south Texas there are not many cities. Just Highway 90 that we ran along for most of the trip through the state. John, in the club car, also acted as our travel guide giving us interesting facts about some of the towns we passed by. What movies had been filmed there or where Judge Roy Bean held court. Most trains did not add commentary to the ride. In mid-morning we passed through a thunder storm as I watched lightning bolts crash the prairie. It did not last long and the weather was nice the remainder of the state.

There was a couple I had seen the day before, but had not talked to yet. They turned out to be a couple of the more interesting people I would meet on any train. The husband and wife were in their mid-40's. They were from Great Britain and were taking a year to go around the world! They had seen the east coast and now were heading west and would spend time on the west coast before going to Australia and New Zealand. They were very interested my trip and they told me some about theirs. I don't think they had been to Texas before. I also ended up sitting with them at lunch. Their property in London backed up to Regents Park. I would guess it was pricey real estate. If I got their names I did not record them. It would have been fun to look them up and see who they really were. I had been to London twice and told them I had seen the Queen, etc. I had also just finished a Churchill biography by Boris Johnson (mayor of London). I'm not sure if that impressed them or not. They never displayed their politics. The theme of the Churchill book was that he was the right person for that time in history. We talked about Lincoln, the Civil War, and other things about US History. Mrs. asked me if I had any other interesting things on a bucket list. I said I would like to find a place where I could sit all night and watch the Milky Way. I had seen it many times, but always in passing. I never sat out with an objective just to observe. There must be the best time of the year where our night sky is facing the center of the galaxy. That would be my planned time. Anywhere. Plus, no moon. In hearing that they offered for me to come to Nepal when they visited in March. The Milky Way was spectacular there. Seems they had started a school in Nepal and visited in yearly. I did not take them up on their offer. I think I may have been speechless by this bit of information.

The train must have been a little ahead of schedule as we had a longer stop in Alpine, Texas. Alpine is the county seat of Texas' largest county. It is close to the entrance of Big Bend National Park. After lunch we reached El Paso. We had at least 20 minutes there and it was a nice day to take a walk. The depot was one of the classic depots and was designed by the same person who designed Washington's Union Station. We were right next to athletic fields for the UTEP (University of Texas at El Paso). Also, we were right across the street from Mexico and Ciudad Juarez. I probably could have gotten closer for some pictures, but upon leaving the station we ran parallel to the border and crossed the Rio Grande as it came down from New Mexico. I ran my video camera as we left El Paso. The other side of the fence (yes, there is a fence) was quite bleak. No paved streets. There were several "facilities" that looked like prisons. The fence headed west, up over a mountain and out of sight as we left the border and headed toward Deming, New Mexico. Meanwhile, about this time I received a text from my brother in Seattle. "Thanks for the camera", the text read.

I wanted to plan my dinner time so I could get out when we got to Tucson. However, we ended up stopping there while I was eating dinner. My cousin Pete lives in Tucson. But since I had not planned a stop there I had not contacted him. I now wish I had as I had not seen him in quite a while, and it would have been nice to be able to say hello. I had the chicken for dinner and ate with a retired Marine and his wife. He had a USMC hat, so I knew he was a Marine. They were a nice couple to talk with. He was in his 80's and had served in Korea.

I was already nearing my second night on the train. Since we were scheduled to arrive in Los Angeles at 5:35am most people wanted to turn in early. I was okay in having my bed set up early. I had already rearranged my bag so I would need minimal time in the morning to depart the train. I still had one more bottle of wine, but decided to save it. It was not used until my first night out of Seattle heading east again. We would be entering California and go through Palm Springs and Pomona in the middle of the night. I'm not sure if I slept any better than the prior night. However, we were in for a surprise as we reached LA about an hour early! Not only that they wanted everyone off the train by 5:30am.

Amtrak at Alpine, Texas, Station

Los Angeles Layover

Oh joy, I got to sit in the LA depot until after 10:00 when my train up the coast departed. I found an open Subway. However, the only way to get Wi Fi was to purchase it from Amtrak. So, I paid $1.99 for an hour of internet time and updated my Facebook. I saw an email asking for some anecdotes for my friend Dana. Dana was a neighbor of ours in Indiana and would be turning 60. We had known each other since 1987. His daughter was putting together some stories about her dad. It was needed fairly quickly and I did not know how much time I would have in the next couple of days so I drafted some stories and emailed them to Connie so she could pass along. That did help pass some time.

The LA depot was uncomfortable and somewhat crowded. There were several local trains leaving from the station and the main waiting hall was hot. Two, big, six-foot fans were in place to try to cool the space down. And this was at six in the morning. I moved seats a couple of times as other people left seats that were closer to the fans. However, when I made a restroom run I lost my seat. I didn't want to check my bag so I had that to contend with. I watched people who I had traveled with me from New Orleans arrange their LA transportation, including the English couple. There were big "flip" boards for all the trains and I watched my next train (#14 Coastal Starlight) slowly move up toward the top of one board and then finally up the "closer to departure" column. I would need a seat assignment, which was discouraging as that meant the train would be full. I was back in coach. When I was only be going as far as Oakland the arrival time would be at 9:24pm. However, when I heard that cousin Mickey would not be in Oakland I changed my reservation to go all the way to Portland. That now meant a 29-hour leg and another night sleeping in coach. At least it would be my last in coach. However, it did mean three straight nights on trains after leaving New Orleans. I don't know how so many people got window seats before me, but I wanted a window on the left side (to see the ocean) but got the very front row and a right-side window. I would see the ocean from the dome car.

Leg 10
#14 Coast Starlight
September 25-26
Los Angeles to Portland   1,190 Miles   29:07 Hours
States: California, Oregon

Once we started out I only stayed in my seat long enough to have the conductor take my ticket. I then went to the dome car where I spent the next two hours to get pictures from of Los Angeles to the coast. I did meet my seat mate. He was someone I labeled the "Gay Australian". Another person I wish I had a picture of. He was wearing all black with a sleeveless vest and cowboy hat and various ear ornaments. I could not do justice to his accent. He was on his way to San Francisco with friends, who were elsewhere on the train. Very interesting to talk with, however, he didn't spend much time at his seat. He hung out in the club car with his friends. Across from me I met a young lady as she settled into the window seat. She was a college student from Canada and was also doing an extended rail trip. She would go as far as Sacramento, where she would then catch the Zephyr back toward Chicago. She was soon joined by the "whiner" in the aisle seat. The whiner had the voice of Moaning Myrtle from the second Harry Potter movie. She had multiple bags and it took her some time to stow everything with my help. She then begged Miss Canada to trade seats. The whining started. "I get claustrophobic if I can't see out a window. I really need a window seat. Every time I travel I get motion sickness and looking out helps me." (Imagine the whining voice). Young Miss Canada held her ground and refused to move. So, Whiner resigned herself to being sick. She would just have to find a window elsewhere.

The ride out of Los Angeles and up the California coast was what I imagined an Amtrak ride should look like. It was a beautiful day and once we hit the coast we went along the ocean for a couple of hours. In LA itself I saw Dodger Stadium, Burbank Airport (now Bob Hope Airport), and the Los Angeles River (a really big storm sewer). I sat in the dome car and made conversation with other passengers. Some knew all the landmarks and others were traveling this territory for the first time. There was a man from Tucson, who I would see for the next 24 hours. He was interesting to listen to. He was retired and lived out in the desert of Arizona "off the grid". He had hiked virtually every trail worth hiking in the west. He was talking with a man who also had extensive hiking background. He was an archeologist who was published. They would digress into discussions about some of their hikes and totally ignore the geography we were passing at the time. I could only take so much of their conversation. Then there was the young man who was enthralled with something on his laptop. He rarely looked out the window as he knew where we were going. Seems he was developing a "Pet Pal" type website and was hoping to release it soon. That is probably not the correct name, but something of that nature. He worked for Martin Marietta and was doing this on the side. Probably hoping one of the internet giants would discover and like his design and pay him millions. You never know.

There were miles of beaches going north out of LA toward Santa Barbara. Lots of public beaches with picnic areas and other places to park RV's. Off shore you could see oil platforms. I took video of some of the ride. We made good time and everyone was in good spirits. The train passed through Vandenberg Air Force Base where the Air Force does some missile testing and launches. We passed through some agricultural areas with considerable irrigation. With the terrible water shortage in the state it was interesting to see how much water still needed to go for crops. Since I was no longer in a sleeper my meals were not included. My lunch was a sandwich from the club car. The young lady who ran the club car on this route was new with Amtrak. I told her she needed to meet John (her counterpart on the Sunset Limited). She was looking for an approach to help her market the club car services.

I had never been this far up the California Coast before. I had been south from Monterey along Big Sur, but not north out of LA. A real treat was seeing the very nice town of San Luis Obispo. We had an extended stop there (smoke break) so I got out to walk around. When rail lines pass above the back yard of homes you usually see properties that are run down and upkeep is not the best. (Except the Minnesota lake homes). I did not see one "below average" property coming into this town. I could live in any of the houses I saw from the train.

Another treat was the scenery as the train left San Luis Obispo and slowly climbed a mountain range. There were horseshoe turns where we could see the front half of the train. The terrain was large rolling hills with scattered oak trees. I love the parts of California that look like that. Once over the summit we were headed toward Casa Robles, Soledad, and on to Salinas. In this area was a lot more agriculture. A lot more. I could not tell what was growing in the hundreds acres of fields we passed. It looked like it could be lettuce and similar produce. Some fields were entirely covered in plastic sheets with only the plant coming up. It seems it was all very labor intensive, including the control of irrigation. Also, orchards of various fruits or nuts. I did not see any vineyards, but they are in that same area.

By the time we reached San Jose it was dark. I don't recall my dinner that night. There was a very large stadium we passed in the San Jose area that I was not able to determine its name or team affiliation. I don't believe it was Levi Stadium the new home of the 49ers. We then proceeded up the east side of the bay. Back in 1976-77 we lived in Hayward for about 8 months and worked in San Francisco. I recognized some of the Bart Stations by name and location. We were to have arrive in Oakland around 9:25pm. By this time Miss Canada was sitting next to me as the Australian was still hanging out with friends and Miss Whiner seemed to have taken over both seats for her stuff and her attempt at napping. Miss Canada was from Eastern Canada and was just seeing the country. She had a rail pass that tied in Canadian travel with US. She seemed very independent and did not mind traveling on her own. She would get off in Sacramento, spend the night at a student hostel and then depart on an east bound train in the morning.

Going into the Oakland rail yard, which appeared to be one of the major Amtrak yards, I noticed an old private rail car that was lit. People were dining in the car as it sat alone on a siding. The car was very old and obviously had been renovated. I found out the next morning that while we were stopped in Oakland they attached the private car to the rear of our train. We pulled them as far as Oregon. Seems Amtrak will pull private cars. It would be interesting to know the cost. As I mentioned from a couple of prior delays we are often not told much when we just sat somewhere. In this case the Oakland station. I had wanted to stay awake to see the ride up to Sacramento. I used to make that drive a lot and was interested in the bridge we would cross in Martinez near a mothballed fleet of navy ships. However, we just sat in Oakland. For two hours. There were no announcements as the reason of the delay. We found out from someone that a car (automobile) had been abandoned on the tracks outside the station and it took that long to have it removed. AAA must have been busy doing other things on a Friday evening.

Once we got going it was now very late in getting to Sacramento. Miss Canada had planned on walking to the Hostel as it was close. They did allow people to come in at any time of the night which was a relief to her. The platform at Sacramento was packed. I don't think I had seen any other station in the middle of a route so full of people. And it was about 2:00 in the morning. I said good bye to Miss Canada. A lady did get on who shared her seat with Miss Whiner. They seemed to work things out okay despite all the stuff being stored on that side of the aisle. I think I may have had some of the overflow above me. I lucked out and had no companion. But, that did not help my sleep. I remember Chico about 4:00 in the morning and by the time we reached Shasta I was basically up. At one point the train made a stop in the mountains of Northern California, before we reached Dunsmuir. The conductor came quickly through our car heading for the back of the train. It was still dark. A few minutes later I saw a light outside moving along the train. It was the conductor, with a flashlight walking along the train looking along the rail bed and under the cars. About five minutes later we started moving again. As usual there was no explanation. It was still official "sleep time" so they wouldn't make a night announcement anyway. We must had hit something and they needed to determine what it was.

It was unlikely we were going to make up the time we had lost the night before. Our arrival in Portland was planned for 3:30, but it looked more like it was going to be 5:00 or after. My cousin Butch was to meet me and then we had a three-hour drive to his brother's place in Depoe Bay, on the Oregon Coast. It would be another late arrival. After breakfast I went to the observation car to watch sunrise and the nice scenery around Mt. Shasta and into southern Oregon. We had good views of Mt. Shasta from south to north. It was a challenge to get pictures as the mountain ducked in and out of trees. I was joined by the Tucson passenger and some others. Again, I listened to tales of various hiking trails in the west and somehow we never seemed to get on the subject of where we were at that moment. Again, the conversation soon tired me out and I went back to my seat for quiet and to cat nap.

By early afternoon I was talking to my cousin. I threw out the idea of him meeting me in Salem. He could get an hour of driving out of the way and I would just get off the train a couple of stops early. No rule against that and I had all my bags with me. I had a feeling that we would be virtually driving right past this station in a couple of hours so we could save a lot of time. Butch said that he would rather get me at the Portland depot. Oh well. We'd have more time to talk as we had not seen each other in over 25 years. I think he wanted to watch the Oregon Football game on TV. When our train went through Eugene, I saw students walking to the stadium and game. I had watched Oregon play Washington there in 1972.

The Whiner and her new seat companion wanted to join me for lunch in the dining car. Maybe my discomfort showed as her companion (a woman my age), was concerned with the menu and cost. I went over the options for both the dining car and the club car and they decided to get something from the club car. I was not offended. I should also point out that Whiner was wearing pajama bottoms, or sweats whose pattern resembled pajama bottoms. She was always getting stuff down and putting it back from the bag storage above her seat. Every time she reached up her bottoms would slip down revealing a little too much of her behind than proper. This is not like telling someone their zipper is down, so I didn't really say anything because as soon as her hands dropped and she turned around she was okay. I just wondered how many passengers behind me had a similar view. She was also getting off in Portland. Among her rambling was saying she had not seen her kids, (who had to be little based on her age), in a while. She provided just enough information to get your interest, but without any background information I had no idea what she was talking about. The ultimate came shortly before we arrived in Portland. She stood in the aisle and went into great detail to me about how hard it was to wash her hair. (It was very long brown hair that she was always pulling it around). It had no body and got quite oily. Here again, I would have loved to know what the people behind me were observing. I was just thankful that my travel with her was almost at an end. When I left her as she was working on getting about four bags off the train.

The view into Portland, as most places along the west coast was very nice. We went along the Willamette River, which I knew to be one of the few rivers in the country that flowed northerly. It emptied into the Columbia just outside of Portland. Mt. Hood was visible to the northeast and we were soon in the Portland Union Station. My cousin, Richard (Butch) was to pick me up. We had not seen each other since my brother's wedding in 1987. Butch is 7 years older than me. He was born right at the start of the war. Growing up he lived with our grandparents until about the time our grandmother died. He then moved to Portland where his mom was by this time. I have a lot of childhood memories that include Butch. He lost his wife, Carol, to cancer a few years ago. He was outside the depot with his Yukon and little dog. We then figured out how to get out of the city and were heading south toward Salem, where we would cut over to the Oregon Coast and Depoe Bay.

Depoe Bay, Oregon Stay

Butch's older brother Chuck (Mickey) has a very nice house in a gated community near Depoe Bay. I had visited him there in 2013 and knew it was a good place to "chill out". The house has three levels with a view over a cove that then extends to the ocean. It is not right on the beach, but it is a short walk and the ocean is within sight. The main level has a two-level ceiling over the living area, a nice kitchen and the master bedroom. The lower level has two more big bedrooms (both connected to a large bath), and a TV room that could also be a small bedroom. The upper level has a loft that overlooks the living room and out to the ocean. It can double as another bedroom. Mickey has also converted a long storage area into an office.

When we got there I met Mickey's daughter Jeanine and her husband Mark. They usually spend a month there in the fall and were just finishing up their stay. I had not seen Jeanine since the mid-60's that I remember. There was plenty of room for everyone and we had a late dinner of pork chops and I settled in to a nice shower and the first good sleep I had had since New Orleans. I arrived on Saturday evening and would be there until Wednesday, when I headed to Seattle.

Sunday morning was a very nice day. Not a cloud in the sky type of day and gentle breezes. We had breakfast at a place in Newport, and sat by the window overlooking the ocean. Breakfast included Mickey, Butch and me. We then spent about an hour in the town of Newport. There is a very scenic bridge that takes the coast highway over the entrance of the harbor. Then in the town you see the basic tourist attractions with gift shops and a "Ripley's Believe it or Not". In the harbor were scores of fishing boats and there were some piers and canneries where fresh fish were being transferred or sorted for sale. Some of the tanks were full of large crabs. Out on the finger piers was the sound of sea lions. By following the noise we came across from 50 to 100 sea lions on floating platforms just hanging out. Many were sleeping and others trying to sleep. I had seen a similar assemblage of these animal's at Fisherman's Warf in San Francisco several times. We could have watched them all day, but we had other places to see. There is a lighthouse (Yaquina) that is managed by the National Park system near Newport. For some reason I had decided to bring my National

Park pass with me on the trip, so we all got in for free. More beautiful views up and down the coast were had from the lighthouse grounds.

Mickey's son Clayton also lives in Depoe Bay. He owns a bar with his wife. We found him home and visited for a while. Oregon allows medical marijuana for personal use. Clayton had the legal four plants in the back of his house. His dad had to show me. Go figure. After we got home we had steaks on the grill and watched the Seahawks on TV.

Monday, we had breakfast at home and Butch and I drove up the coast to Tillamook. Here is another place I had not been for about 50 years. Tillamook is famous for its cheese. In 1933 there was a huge forest fire (called the Tillamook Burn) between the ocean and Portland. I recall, as a kid, driving through the area and still seeing remnants of the forest fire. This was a nice day for a drive. We then did the self-tour of the cheese factory and had lunch in their cafeteria. I bought some cheese to give to some of my Seattle visits coming up later in the week. We then drove a little more up the coast to Garibaldi, which is a favorite fishing spot for my cousins. I think Butch realized that I was not really into fishing anymore and we then returned home.

From Mickey's house there are foot trails that take you to the beach. All the homes along the ocean are up on a bluff about 50 feet above the water. A high natural rock wall runs along the entire development below the homes to the water. It is impossible to be on the beach except where there are coves. The half-mile path along the top of the bluff gives very nice views of the ocean. So, I took a walk to take some pictures. The whales had been running this week and yet I didn't see any. One clue as to where they are is the presence of whale watching boats out of Depoe Bay Harbor that follow pods as they move south along the coast. There were no boats that day. However, it was a very nice day for a walk.

That evening we went to dinner at a Mexican place right next to the famous Depoe Bay highway bridge. Seems appropriate to go to the Oregon Coast and have Mexican. We would make up for it the next night. Since it was Monday we watched football that evening. Jeannine and Mark had left and we were on our own for meals and found no one knew how to fix the cable if someone hit a wrong button on the remote. A bunch of old cousins that the simple technology of watching TV had passed us by.

Tuesday would be my last full day on the coast. It was very foggy in the morning. Mickey had to take his truck in for servicing at Newport. That afternoon while looking out the window toward the ocean I noticed whale watching boats. Sure enough, I could see some "blows" as whales surfaced. I decided to take my video camera back to the ocean view walking path and was not disappointed. There were several groups of whales in sight at any time. Some had just two or three whales and others had more. They would all surface within seconds of each other and many times do a roll where their fin and tail came out of the water. My goal was to catch some of this action on my video camera. I probably shot 20 minutes in total and got some good whale shots. Now I just need to figure out how to edit out all the time where I was just taping water with no whales. There was a high fog layer, so it was easy to look out to the west with no sun glare. Some whales were close to the shore and I could hear them when they blew. Not a bad bonus for my trip. That evening we went to Mo's in Lincoln City and I had Fish & Chips. Their menu had the option of cod or halibut, with the halibut being $3.00 more. My cousins pretty much told me I was to get the halibut. It was good.

Finally, on Wednesday morning I was on my way again. Butch and I left Depoe Bay early and had breakfast at a very small town called Otis. The Cafe was about the only thing there beside a bait shop and post office that I saw in Otis. Three months later it is the only place where I charged something on my trip that did not hit my credit card. I had a 12:15 train and we got to Portland in plenty of time. It was nice being able to spend time with these cousins. Too much time goes by between seeing some family members.

Leg 11
September 30
#506 Amtrak Cascades
Portland to Seattle   187 Miles   3:50 Hours
States: Oregon, Washington

The Portland to Seattle run is an extension of Amtrak and called the Amtrak Cascades. They run about five trains a day between Portland and Seattle and service many other northwest towns on side routes. The equipment is different than the regular Amtrak trains. The cars are more commuter in type so there is not a section of sleeper cars. The seats are not quite as spacious. However, there was a club car to get food and snacks. The cars had TV monitors that kept passengers posted as to our speed and next destination. There were also trivia questions about the area we were going through. Not only that the ride was very scenic. We crossed the Columbia River into Washington State north of Portland. Running basically parallel to Interstate 5 there was a lot of scenery I was familiar with. I was just seeing it from a different vantage point. The top speed of this train was 79 miles an hour. I found out form a conductor on the Empire Builder the next week that 79 was the top approved speed for any Amtrak train. That seems about right. We made some good speeds, but I never felt we were going any faster than 80.

I started paying more attention to the scenery after we left Olympia. About 60 miles south of Seattle the state capital is on the southern end of Puget Sound. I knew we would be passing the Chambers Bay Country Club where the 2015 US Open was held. It should be easy to spot as there was considerable TV coverage of that event. I had my video camera ready to shoot the entire course as we passed by. There are no second chances on these trains. On this day a mile-long freight train blocked the view of most of the course. Had we been on a double decker it would have been fine, but not from ground level. So much for that. However, I did see some of the course and got an appreciation of the scenery of the Sound. Several miles further up the coast we approached the Tacoma Narrows. This was the location of the suspension bridge that crashed down in 1946 due to heavy winds and a major design flaw. This is the only bridge crossing of Puget Sound. The only other options to get to the Olympic Peninsula are to take a ferry boat or drive all the way to Olympia. The ferry boats are frequent and depart from multiple locations around Seattle. A new bridge was built in the late 40's which I was very familiar with. My cousins lived in Port Orchard (just south of Bremerton) and we made the drive through Tacoma and over the bridge once a month during my entire youth. My dad would not pay the money for the ferry and the departure times were not always a time saver anyway. Now there was a second bridge next to the one built in the 40's. Goes to show how much traffic is now going to the peninsula as many people now live there and commute into Seattle and Tacoma. The farm my cousins lived on is now a "Park and Ride". I'm not sure if it is for the Seattle Ferry or busses to Tacoma, or both.

I got some good pictures of the bridges despite my limited camera capability. After the bridge we swung around into downtown Tacoma. Tacoma has never been a scenic city. It has a large container port with a river coming into the bay. There was also pulp mills going way back which made the town smell. The downtown was never big. There is a domed stadium (Tacoma Dome) that I had only seen from the interstate. The train did not go directly north toward Seattle from there. Instead to went more east toward Puyallup. The good part of that was very nice views of Mt. Rainier. This is a huge volcano that we saw out our kitchen window in Seattle where I grew up. However, from Puyallup we were 40 miles closer. While it was a clear, sunny day, it was somewhat hazy so the pictures I got were not real sharp. The train then went through the Kent Valley and into Seattle along Boeing Field. There is a lot of aviation history located at this two-mile-long airfield and assembly plants. I would visit the museum there in a few days.

Seattle Stay

Seattle is where I grew up and spent the first 28 years of my life. It is always nice to get back. Connie and I lost all four of our parents during a 10-month period in 2004-05. Since then my visits have spaced out to every few years instead of several a year. Even with all those visits I found there were many people who I had not had a chance to see in years. I wanted to focus this visit on seeing friends and family.

So, finally into Seattle's Union Station. This was the first time I had visited this station since I took trains home from college. It was not the best time of day to arrive in Seattle. The city is very congested at rush hour and my train arrived on time at 4:05. I would be staying at my brother's house in West Seattle and he met me to take me to the closest Enterprise Rental Car. It just so happens that is in the heart of downtown so John and I headed right into the busy 4:00 traffic. Lots of busses service the downtown, so navigation was slow. Once I got my car I had to fight my way back out of the city. I went down Second Avenue. Traffic had to wait through a couple of light changes at each intersection (every block), and I finally made it to the Columbia Street on ramp to the Alaskan Way Viaduct. That would be less than 15 minutes to my brother's house. The viaduct is very old and has two levels, one north and the other south. Before the interstate was finished in 1967 it was the only express way to get through the city from north to south. The entire length is now being moved underground so I immediately ran into construction. However, I soon was in my home neighborhoods of West Seattle.

My brother lives in a house that is down the street from where we grew up. His wife Shawne and their two kids, Anika and Nick, have had this house as their only family home. John likes German Shepherds and I was greeted by two as I arrived. Growing up this was a house where a couple of my friends lived and I had first been in this house in the mid 50's. Lee Dennison had polio and I recall visiting him in his bedroom when he recovered from a leg surgery. I think that was the same room where I would be staying. Anika (I used her room) was away at school and I would see her the next day.

I mentioned earlier in this narrative that I wanted to see Nick play in a high school football game. He was now a senior and I would see him play on Saturday afternoon. After Nick got home from practice (where a teammate suffered a broken wrist) we had pork chops (coincidence I'm sure) and went up to Nick's school (Seattle Lutheran) to see the weight room. The renovation of this room had become Nick's service project to the school. An old "Girls Locker Room" had been converted to a weight room for the football team and other high school athletes. This is very small school. The football team plays "8 Man" and there are only about 20 boys that suit up for games. This weight room would be his legacy to the school and he was very proud of his efforts. It looked like his mom and dad also deserved a lot of credit for their time commitment in getting this room converted.

A replacement body for my camera was waiting for me at my brothers. It took a different battery and photo card than my old model, but it came with a battery and charger. Shawne had an extra photo card. I transferred the lens and strap and was good to go. A new camera for the rest of the trip.

The next day would be Thursday and I would be meeting my old college friend Sue to go up to Western Washington University to visit our old campus. I have already mentioned that I had not seen Sue since the early 80's from my best memory. Sue was my roommate Byron's girlfriend. They went out together from 1969 on-and-off until the mid-70's. I saw her a lot during that time, and I was often her driver to go home for a weekend or to visit Byron when he lived in Corvallis, Oregon for two years during that time. Sue was no longer married to Mike. She was living in a house in Sammamish, which is on the east side of Lake Sammamish between Issaquah and Redmond. When we still lived near there this area was mostly forest with a few roads through the woods. She lives just a block up from the lake. I was to pick her up around 8:00am so we could make Bellingham before 10:00. My niece Anika is a sophomore there and we would meet up with her for a modern-day tour until she had to go to class.

After Sue found me on Facebook, we started a daily correspondence regarding our college lives. She had kept a diary of those days and she was full of questions as to what I recalled about events or people. She was also going through all her photographs and trying to scan them so she would have them saved digitally. I was able to help her as I have done quite a bit of photo restoration myself with our family photos. She sent me a few pictures before I left on my trip that I was able to identify people, restore some of the color, or crop to bring in details better. However, I soon realized that if a picture had a white frame around it she wanted it left that way. I also was able to scan a slide for her, a very good picture of her and Byron. She had pictures of me and Connie and even with Julee, the girl I dated before I met Connie in 1972. It was fun to try to reconstruct our college days. Visiting the campus would also bring back memories.

After Connie and I got married in 1973 I only recall visiting the campus twice. I was there around 1992 or 93 with my son John. He was in the first grade and was impressed that I had to live at my school. I visited again around 2002 with my daughter Kristin and my aunt Sara. Kristin was a student at Indiana University by this time. As Sara was over 80 at the time she was not up for much walking, so I probably didn't get to see as much as I had wished.

So, after meeting Sue again we headed for Bellingham. The time flew by as we had a lot to catch up on. When we got to the school we found things had changed a lot. Like where to park. I recalled where the visiting lots were the last time I was there. However, that was now new athletic facilities. I finally got Anika on the phone and she directed me to a lot where she was parking for the day. We found her as she was paying for her spot. Anika is a very shy girl and over the next hour of touring the main campus we did much more talking than she did. Every building or lecture hall had a story or memory.

After Anika left us to go to class we walked to the upper campus where our dorms were. I lived in Ridgeway Beta and Sue was in a neighboring dorm, Ridgeway Gamma. At both dorms we ran into very friendly Resident Aids who wondered what a couple of old folks were doing around their dorms. These dorms were now 50 years old and appeared to be in very good condition. I could see them lasting another 50 years. Everywhere we went to look we were reminded of stories or people. It was a very nice day and I got some good pictures.

Bellingham is located 90 miles north of Seattle, 20 miles from Canada, and 50 miles south of Vancouver. Victoria, on Vancouver Island, is further south than Bellingham. The town has a population of about 85,000 people so it is a fair size. The student population is between 9 and 10,000. The state university is a very good liberal arts school and produces many of the Washington State teachers. While the student population has not changed much since the 60's there are a lot more buildings on campus. Some of the long-term buildings are old and probably did not have the resources needed for university departments. Where athletic fields used to be are now buildings and nice, newer sports facilities are further out from the center of campus.

After leaving the campus we took the drive up to Sehome Hill. The highest point in the city has beautiful views that are now obstructed by trees. We could see Mt. Baker, and the water to the west through gaps in the trees. As students we were probably not all that interested in the view, so I really don't recall how much it had changed. Landmarks in the town used to be the bars that were hangouts for the students. I didn't recognize any names or locations. Likewise, we had a hard time finding any non-fast food place to eat and finally settled on a café in a strip mall. Such is progress. Going home we went along the coast of the Sound via old Chuckanut Drive and visited Larrabee State Park. Some of Sue's old pictures were taken there.

Back home Sue had a chicken cooking in a crock pot all day which we ate while watching Thursday Night Football. Seems like I didn't miss as many games as I thought I would.

I saw another long-lost cousin on Friday. Ron Lidstrom was named for my dad. He is the youngest of Pete's (now in Tucson), four kids. After Connie and I moved away in 1976 I doubt we ever saw him again. Maybe at my brother or sisters' weddings. I just don't recall. Ron is now in his mid-40's and is a foreman of a long-term construction project in the Smith Tower. The Smith Tower was the tallest building west of the Mississippi when it was built in 1912. It is still an attractive building for small firms to occupy and they are renovating the tower a couple floors at a time before new tenants move in. I got a "behind the scenes" tour of some of the renovation work and we had lunch in an Irish Pub that is located in the first floor. When I was a kid my dad took me to the observation deck on the top floor. That was in the late 50's. By 1962 the Space Needle and some of the first tall office towers were being built and the tower is now dwarfed by much taller building. However, it was interesting to see something now over 100 years old still function in its original purpose.

I had parked a few blocks away and realized that the garage would be a good location to park for the Mariners game I would be attending that evening. So back to Sammamish and pick up Sue for the game. We met Byron at the Pyramid Ale House, across from the stadium. This was an interesting meeting. Byron and Sue dated through much of college and beyond, yet they eventually married other people. I was in Byron's wedding in 1977, in West Newton, Pa. He married Margie, who was supposed to join us at the game, but ended up having to babysit grandkids. I think Sue married Mike in 1976, just before we moved to California. The couples ran in the same circles for a couple of years and the girls worked in the same Seattle hospital. However, Sue and Mike transferred to Spokane and at that point dropped out of sight. Sue and Byron had not seen each other for over 35 years, (seems to be a common theme, I know), nor had they had any contact as far as I know. Since Byron does not do Facebook he had been missed when Sue started looking for old friends. So, sitting at the game was a little awkward at times, but we all survived the evening.

Besides talking we did actually watch the ballgame. It was two days before the end of the season, so this was Fan Appreciation Night. Fireworks after the game and a lot of giveaways. The M's won. There was a light rain that evening so the roof was closed at Safeco Field during the game. By the end of the game the rain had stopped and in time for fireworks the roof was opened and we had a good show.

Saturday was back to nice weather. Nicks game was at West Seattle Stadium. I played YMCA flag football on this same field in 1960. The stadium had probably been around from the 30's or 40's. It was no longer big enough to be used for high school games for Seattle schools, but is fine for a small school like Lutheran. It has old covered wooden bleachers. Just outside the west fence is an area set up for high school track and field events. Shot put and discus. That was where my little league field was in 1961. The east end of the field sits up above the back nine of the West Seattle Golf Course and has a great view of downtown Seattle. Trees were trying to block this view as well. In 5th and 6th grade the track was the location of "Field Days" where all the elementary schools in West Seattle competed in races, jumping, and other activities. I represented Genesee Hill both years.

Lutheran lost the game in the final few minutes, but I don't think they lost again until well into the state tournament. With such a small squad many of the players literally played the entire game. They were exhausted when the game ended. I like the fact that a small school makes it possible for every kid to play. But, oh my, what a workout. This was homecoming and Nick came out of the locker room at halftime to escort one of the senior princesses. One golf cart made a lot of trips to bring all the girls and their escorts to their spots in front of the grandstands. There was a dance that night, but I didn't hear much about that. We had sloppy Jo's for dinner and watched Norte Dame Football.

Sunday was another very nice day. I met Connie's nephew Jim Cotton and his five-year-old daughter Elsie for brunch near his place on Capitol Hill. It was a fun visit. Jim is three weeks older than my daughter Kristin and he was raised in Germany in US schools. We saw him every summer when he visited, usually with Connie's folks. They lived in Germany from 1978 to 1994. Turns out Jim's girlfriend worked at the restaurant, so I had a chance to meet her as well. They are now engaged. Elsie kept calling me Uncle Bruce and I corrected to say "Great Uncle Bruce".

On the way home I stopped to take scenery pictures you never take when you live somewhere. It was a very pretty and clear day, so I took pictures of the Sound, the City, Alki Beach, and old play area's overlooking the Sound. We took these views for granted as kids. We didn't realize how special they were. We could see two National Parks from our house. Mt. Rainier and Olympic. Not too many places can make that claim.

For dinner I drove over to Kirkland and met up with Brad and Sue W. They were our next-door neighbors when we had our first house in in Lynnwood 1975. We moved away in 1976 and kept in touch over the years, mostly via Christmas card letters. I think I last saw them in the mid-80's with my daughter Kristin. We met at Anthony's overlooking Lake Washington for a nice salmon dinner. Brad just retired from 40 plus years at Pac-Car. He was in their accounting area. We all looked older, but it is amazing how you can resume old acquaintances after that much time and how personalities don't change much.

One more full day in Seattle. Monday, I spent with my high school buddy Danny L. I had seen Dan at my 20th reunion in 1987. Then when my dad died in 2005, Dan called me after seeing the obituary in the paper. On all my Seattle visits since then I have stayed with him and his wife Mary. His extra space (kind of a basement apartment), was not available on this trip as their daughter was visiting from Norway, where she has been working and doing post graduate study. Glad I had a "Plan B". Dan and I met early and had breakfast at one of my parents favorite places, Huckleberry Square in Burien. We then went to the Flight Museum at Boeing Field. I had been there twice before and it had grown a lot. Outdoors is the very first 747, President Kennedy's Air Force One, a Supersonic Transport, and a test model of the Dreamliner. Plus, a lot of military planes like the B-47. Danny and I share a lot of high school memories, so it is always fun to meet up with him.

On Tuesday afternoon I would board my last train east. I had some time to kill so went to see Sue again. We drove around her area and I saw a school I substituted at in 1974. Her son went to Jr. High School there. I found where my sister used to live about five miles to the north. They moved away six or seven years ago, so it was just a challenge of how lost I could get in a maze of streets and forest. After lunch I headed back to Seattle and returned the rental car. At 2:00 in the afternoon the traffic was very easy and Enterprise drove me down an empty 2nd Ave. to Union Station. What more could I ask for.

Leg 12
October 6-8
#8 Empire Builder
Seattle to St. Cloud, MN   1,719 Miles   34:35 Hours
States: Washington, Idaho, Montana, North Dakota, Minnesota

My train would leave at 4:40 so I had plenty of time. I had a sleeper car on this route, however, I was only able to get a berth on the lower level. Not terrible, but I liked being up higher on the other trains. I would be spending two nights on the train. Now that we were into October, sunset was coming early and I would be denied some scenery of the Washington Cascades and the Rockies west of Glacier as it would not be light. I missed the crowds by traveling this time of the year, but didn't have as much daylight.

In reading back through all my notes and my drafts of this narrative I realize that the upcoming last leg of the trip would not match my expectations. The northern route was the trip that got my interest on this whole trip in the first place. Now it was going to be anti-climactic. Some for the reasons described below, but also, I was getting tired of all the train travel. I had great visits in Oregon and Seattle and I realized that this trip allowed me to meet up with many old friends and relatives. I would not have had a chance to do this otherwise, or else I would have at some point over the last 30+ years. The by-product of my travel was the chance to see people. I realized I was ready to get home.

My roomette was on the left side of the train, so I would overlook Puget Sound as we left Seattle. The train goes along the Sound for about 30 miles north to Everett before heading east. Then it follows the old US Highway 2 much of the way. Interesting how the trains and highways have the same right of ways. Most of the way heading north out of Seattle we were right on the water. The day had a very high overcast. That meant that while I would be normally looking into a late afternoon sun, I would not have to worry about sunlight reflecting off the water in my pictures. However, it would also mean that darkness would come earlier as we climbed into the scenic Cascades.

In daylight this leg through the Cascades might be the most scenic of the entire trip. Forest, rivers, high peaks, and tunnels, all made up the next 2 hours before we got to Leavenworth. One tunnel was about

153

8 miles long and took 15 minutes to pass through. I would be eating dinner in the dining car when we reached this tunnel.

Located at the end of my lower level sleeper berth was a sleeping room that went the width of the train. There was no pass through to other cars. There were two men and a woman in the large room and even though I ate with them I really did not get their relationship to each other. The woman was recovering from a medical condition. She had a scarf wrapped around her head like a cancer patient. She was about 40 years of age. It was a challenge for her to walk and we all had to go upstairs for the dining car and observation car. The men (or at least one) was retired from the Navy and they were headed back to Virginia where they lived. I did not ask the reason for their trip as I assumed it had to do with the woman's health. Seattle has a major cancer treatment center. They had not traveled by train before and I advised them of some of things they would experience. For example, they probably could have had the woman's meals delivered. However, I don't think they ever did. They may have brought food back with them a couple of times. So, if she was a cancer patient I was mystified why they all got off the train for a smoke every time they had a chance. Even the woman. Go figure.

Under the description of "I wish I took their picture", were twins on this trip and I had to ask myself if they were for real. Two men about 30. The only thing to tell them apart was their different colored tank tops. With short pants and an Alice in Wonderland Twiddle Dum and Twiddle Dee physical pear body appearance I let my imagination do the rest regarding what they might be like to talk with. They were almost scary. I would expect to see them show up on the internet in the Interesting People You See at Walmart collection.

After my steak dinner I decided I would finally enjoy that bottle of wine I bought in New Orleans. I listened to music after lights went out around Wenatchee. That was before 9:00. I was in bed long before we got to Spokane around 12:45am. We would hold there for about 45 minutes as the train from Portland joined with our train for the rest of the way to Chicago. The ride was smoother than the sleeper that I had out of New Orleans. I was not over the wheels and there was not the lurching of the car as it switched tracks. However, I still did not sleep that well. I probably only got a few hours of good sleep. I knew I could cat nap during the next day to make up some of that sleep.

I was up and awake at 5:45. I got dressed and left the bed down for the porter to fix after he made his rounds. Since I was on the lower level there was plenty of bag storage in the outside hall. I placed my bag there and did not have to use the upper bunk for anything. It was still dark and we were between Libby and Whitefish, Montana. Beyond Whitefish would be Glacier National Park. Breakfast began at 6:30 and only a few people were there that early. I was joined by a man who had boarded the train in Wenatchee and was only going as far as Whitefish. He then would meet a longtime friend and they would do some hiking in the area. He owned a tree service in Wenatchee. I think it included a nursery as well as doing pruning and tree removal. We talked about the terrible fires they had just had in his area that summer and fall. He had a couple of customers who had lost property.

I planned on seeing Glacier from the dome car. I was there right after breakfast and had my choice of seats. It was going to be an overcast day like the day before. Photography would not be the greatest. It would take a while to get totally light. From a moving train I expected to get some blurry pictures as there was not enough light to make the automatic camera use a fast shutter speed. On top of that the windows of the dome car were very dirty. Not much we could do about that. However, it really distracted from the view. I can't believe the windows were washed in Portland, where this car came from. The train went along the southern border of the park and had stops in West Glacier, Essex (Izaak Walton Inn), and East Glacier Park. Leaves were turning on the birch trees giving a pretty yellow to areas of the mountains. We went along a river, but were usually too close and going too fast for good pictures. The dome car was now crowded as people were joining us after eating breakfast. I probably stayed there until about 10:00 when we got out of the mountains. I would have a decent view from my cabin from here on. There was a "three generation" family that I met in the dome car. They were all trying to figure out the best way to take pictures without glare off the glass. I met mom, dad, grandma and a teenage daughter. Seemed like a nice trip for a family to take.

One other observation about Glacier was that I did not see any snow. Even when we got to the east and could look back toward the west there was an absence of snow on any peaks that I saw. It would now take all day to travel across Montana. Big Sky Country. It was the same feeling as crossing Texas, however, I would have no problem

155

telling the two apart if shown pictures. We were in wheat country as well as a lot of hay. I don't recall lunch that last day, but I probably had the burger as it would be my last lunch on the train. One of my companions was a professor type from Seattle. I'm not sure if he was a professor, but he looked and talked like one and seemed to offer an opinion on any topic the table might present. As luck would have it I also sat with him at dinner and I listened as he contradicted himself from our earlier conversations to better please his dinner audience.

I was ready for the trip to be over. I would still have one more night on the train, however, would reach St. Cloud, while it was still dark. In fact, it was dark by the time we reached North Dakota. I had never been to Minot and didn't see anything of it on this trip. Likewise, North Dakota places I had traveled to on business like Devil's Lake, Grand Forks, and Fargo went by unnoticed. After the last meal with Mr. Professor I tried to get to sleep early. If we were on time we would be arriving in St. Cloud at 5:15am. Connie would be staying at the same Best Western we had stayed at a month ago. She was texting me that the train was probably going to be up to an hour late. So not much had changed in the last month regarding this route. If we only had the two hour drive home a lack of sleep would be okay, but we were starting a 20-hour drive to Charlottesville, Virginia to go to our niece, Christina's wedding.

Remember way back on planning this trip I had tried to make the wedding work out and couldn't. It wasn't until the day I booked the tickets that I realized that I could be back in time. Not only that I was hitting my 30-day travel limit right on. A day later and I would have had to buy a 40-day pass for $200 more. The porter and I settled up (tip) and he told me he would still be asleep when I got off, but someone would be rousting me before our St. Cloud arrival. At 5:00am Connie texted me saying the train was due in at about 6:00 am. I was already awake and decided to get my gear packed up and be ready. At about 5:30 the conductor rapped on my door and gave me the 6:00 time. I may have been the only one getting off from his car at 6:00. I met him at the door to our car wished him well and I stepped off the train for the last time.

Wow. I had started out wanting to see the country in a way I had not seen it before. I would say that traveling across Texas and up the California Coast I did that. I also wanted to have a chance to see some friends and family that I don't see that often. In some cases over 30 years. Until I retired I never had the time to visit some of these folks. However, what really enriched the trip was meeting and observing some of the train people. From Mr. CB Radio, to the Gay Australian, to the couple from England, they were all unique. Plane trips are too confining to meet many people and when driving you are limited to who is in your car. I talked to a lot of people who did not even get mentioned. For example, I never mentioned the young Amish couple. I usually told folks I met about the scope of my trip and many said they would like to do something like that if they could. The difference is that "I did".

So, would I do it again? Would I recommend this to others? One thing that worked well for me was the ability to stop and visit folks. Even with some people not available I only spent 10 of the 30 days riding on a train. Most of the time was seeing people. The only hotel expense I had was New Orleans. I would avoid the east coast for any future rail travel. I would consider doing a round trip to Glacier from Minnesota or going all the way to Seattle when the days are longer.

My sister just moved to Colorado Springs. I checked. I can get the California Zephyr in Chicago and stop in Denver and then go on to Sacramento and up the coast again. Maybe Connie would go with me on a trip that short. If so, we will get a bigger sleeper. No more nights in coach.

I would compare the entire trip to the first time I went to Germany and spent three weeks there in 1980. It was special for me. It is something most people will never do. I have always had an appreciation of our country and its diversity. I saw oceans, mountains, desert, prairie, big cities, little towns, and many interesting people. When people said I should "write a book", I thought the trip special enough to warrant this narrative. If any of my great-great-grandkids ever see this I hope they know that I always loved an adventure, and this was a nice one.

Totals: 30 Days   10,342 Miles   223:37 Hours (9 Days, 15 Hours)

Trip Continued. Added states of Iowa and West Virginia.

My train travel ran from September 9th until October 8th. However, I did not actually get back home until October 13th. Of the extra six days we spent four driving. The round trip to Virginia was over 2000 miles over and above the 10,000 I had spent on the train.

We had a wedding to attend. Since moving to Minnesota, we have made the drive back to Indianapolis 4 to 6 times a year. We can make the drive from Marshall in just over 12 hours. It would be a little shorter from St. Cloud. However, we would be driving through Minneapolis-St. Paul during morning rush hour. Then through Wisconsin. We decided to stay away from Chicago and go south from Madison all the way to Bloomington, Illinois. That is an easy, but boring drive with few services. We made it to Indianapolis and our daughter Kristin's place by 6:30 their time (we lost an hour going to Eastern Time). We got to see our grandson Connor and then to bed for an early start the next day to continue the trip.

Friday's drive would only be 9 hours. We were invited to the rehearsal dinner and expected to have a couple of hours to spare after getting there. We cut southeast from Dayton, Ohio and went through West Virginia and on to Charlottesville. So now I got to see Bob and Robyn, Patty and Jim, and Debbie again after just a few weeks. This is the first time that Connie and all four of her siblings were together since our son John's wedding in 2009. Kristin loves to see her cousins and she got to visit a couple she does not see that often. Emily, Tim, Michael, John Cotton, and Christina (the bride) were the only other cousins (out of 15) who could make it. We had a nice dinner in a quaint section of town (I have no idea where we were). Shuttle busses picked us up at the hotel (a Doubletree) and brought us back. A good time to catch up with family.

Most of us met for breakfast in the morning. The wedding would be out at a vineyard that had the ruins of the old estate mansion as a focal point. At some point it had burned down leaving the shell. The location overlooked beautiful vineyards and was a very nice setting. The reception was on the same property. Being at a vineyard we made sure we sampled all their wines. Lots of photos were taken. I let my daughter Kristin do the photo work. I enjoyed not having to worry about pictures yet got copies of hers. Once back at the hotel some cousins stayed up till 2:00. Mom's hate it when even grown kids do that without checking in.

Sunday, we reversed our path back to Indiana and were there by late afternoon. We were staying with Kristin, but went to our son John's home for dinner and to play with Connor. What fun a 20-month-old can be.

We finally had a day to rest. I did my Steak N Shake breakfast and officially took my last picture to post on Facebook. Our friend Chris H brought her twin granddaughters over to John's and we took all the kids to the community play area with swings and climbing forts, etc. The twins are about 4 years old and Connor was watchful of them. That night we went out to dinner and I made a mistake of showing Connor the picture of my dog Luna on my phone. All he wanted to do was call Luna from my phone. "Hi Luna". He finally met Luna in November and now knows where grandpa's dog lives.

Finally, one more 12-hour drive home to Minnesota. I over slept one hour and we did not get on the road until 5:00 am. We still got back in plenty of time to get Luna, Juno, and Wrigley out of the kennel and finally spend a night in my own bed. Now I was really home.

Bruce and Connie near Charlottesville, VA

$\mathbf{B}$**ruce Lidstrom,** a native of Seattle, is now retired from insurance company operations. He has lived in five states and visited the other forty-five. He and his wife, Connie, currently reside in Indiana. They have four children and six grandchildren. This book is dedicated to them. He is also hard at work documenting his family history for future generations.

Printed in the United States
By Bookmasters